Seed of

DAVID

A WORSHIPPER'S GUIDE TO MEND THE HEART AND DISCIPLINE THE FLESH

Published by Godzchild Publications
a division of Godzchild, Inc.
22 Halleck St., Newark, NJ 07104
www.godzchildproductions.net

Printed in the United States of America 2015—First Edition
Cover Design by Maurice Downing

Library of Congress Cataloging-in-Publications Data
Seed of David/ Stephen Hurd

ISBN   978-1-942705-12-3 (pbk.)

1. Hurd, Stephen 2. Worship 3. Life Improvement
4. Instruction 5. Biblical Study

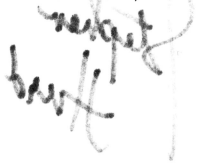

ENDORSEMENTS

"Finally! It's Here! The book we have all been waiting for! This book will challenge yet encourage, prepare and propel all that serve in worship ministry. The wisdom and teaching from this man of God will be treasured for years to come! The table has been spread! Eat and you will be filled!!!"

- Pastor Cassandra Elliott

"The sanctity of worship is restored in this book as Stephen presents the truth of how the enemy has exploited it. Through his personal experiences, he holds nothing back as he urges worship leaders to understand the urgency of their calling for the Kingdom of God. This book needs to be read, not just by worship leaders, but every person who has entered into relationship with Jesus Christ."

- Bishop George Searight
Abundant Life Family

"Stephen Hurd through the literary gem, The Seed of David, presents to us a fresh revelatory insight into the ministry of Praise & Worship. His ability to deal with some tough issues, and present biblical answers, will propel the worship leader into a greater understanding of their role and responsibility, not only in the house of God, but in everyday life as well"

- Dr. Judith McAllister

"There are many questions that people have asked when it comes to the subject of 'Praise & Worship'. But Stephen Hurd skillfully takes you on a journey explaining the obstacles and pitfalls that one may have to encounter when fulfilling the purpose that God has for their life. We may have seen over the years, how worship has changed in the 21st century churches but the chapters in this book will give you guidelines, information and personal experiences on how to genuinely live a life that is Holy before God so that your personal worship time never changes."

- Bishop John Francis
Ruach City Church
(London, UK and Philadelphia, USA)

"A provocative insight for all pastors and worship leaders, Stephen brings a deepened understanding about a part of ministry that is so vital, yet so compromised – the music ministry! From addressing the pitfalls of secularization on God's platform to the essentials needed to bring accuracy to the worship experience, Stephen's wealth of experience, coupled with his heart for God, the church, and his pastor, offers practical solutions to go forward."

- Pastor Bert Pretorius
3C Church
Pretoria, South Africa

TABLE OF CONTENTS

FOREWORD

*L*et everything that has breath praise the Lord. Psalm 150:6. The Psalmist's command is often read and sung in church services all over the world. Praise and worship are essential disciplines to the life and spirit of every Believer. But when you hear these words, do you really know what is being asked of you? Do you fully comprehend all that is required to experience genuine praise and worship? In *Seed of David: A Worshipper's Guide to Mend the Heart and Discipline the Flesh*, Minister Stephen Hurd guides you through the process of understanding and helps you to enter into real worship.

As a renowned Minister of Music and an award-winning recording artist, Minister Hurd knows the significant role that worship plays in both the heart of the church and the hearts of God's people. His experience and insight are evident in every page of this book. He uses practical examples and clear analogies to paint a true and honest picture of what praise and worship are and what they are not. Minister Hurd states: *Praise is the realization of God's faithfulness. Praise is the résumé of experiences that God has proven over time. Worship is when God responds to the praise and celebration offerings we send to Him, and gives us permission to go deeper into a fuller and greater glory of His presence.*

I have had the privilege of serving as Minister Stephen Hurd's pastor. I know first-hand that he lives and breathes the words that he has shared. Praise is in his heart. Worship pours from his soul. And he has a desire to share what he knows with others. In this book, he has done just that.

Whether you are a worship leader or simply desire to experience God's presence more deeply, I encourage you to read *Seed of David*. As you experience God in a new way, you'll be glad that you did.

-Pastor John K. Jenkins, Sr.
Senior Pastor, First Baptist Church of Glenarden

CHAPTER *One*

Building a House of Praise:
Defining Praise

Make a joyful noise unto God, all the earth; sing forth the honor of His name; make his praise glorious. (Psalm 66:1-2)

Whenever a visionary sets out to launch a business, vision, or project, the first thing the organizer must do is come up with the mission statement. The mission statement is the guiding point that helps outsiders, insiders, and team-members to understand the goal of that endeavor. Without a mission, there is no direction. And without direction, your efforts are futile from inception.

If you start building a house without laying a foundation on the ground, you may end up with a beautiful edifice, but the house will not stand for very long. The foundation, like the mission, is the basic thread that connects everything together. In the same way, I think many people in the body of Christ have been trying to "do praise" without knowing the basic mission of this God-ordained gift. I am also of the opinion that we have made praise everything except what it was intended to be. We have made praise about bodily exercise, demonstrative emotions, and fitness routines. But praise is not a choreographed musical interlude that happens during jovial moments in church. Praise is not cantankerous drums beating alongside a B-3 Hammond. Praise is not the ice-breaker to Sunday morning worship. Praise, in its most simplest form, is the spiritual house that God wants to live in within you.

Since the beginning of time, God has always desired to be close to us. For that reason, He built within us an innate desire to be close to him. Like a mother giving birth to a child, there is something in the womb that compels that baby to long not just for a maternal figure, but for the mother herself. There is something that happens during the process of birth that causes a baby to cling onto and desire her parents more than other human beings. This is the similar connection God established with us, his creation, before Adam even knew his maker. That closeness was the first fruit of a relationship between God and man that knew no end or beginning. A timeless affair; a heavenly promise on earth; a dwelling place called praise.

Since the beginning of time, God has always desired to be close to us.

This is why I liken praise to a house. A house is usually owned by its inhabitants and it is furnished for permanent residency. A hotel, however, is owned by an outsider that intends to capitalize from the profit of visitation, without any intention of permanent stay. I wonder, in our quest to become the next great praise leader, or the next great praise dancer, or the next great musician, preacher, or teacher, have we replaced our house for a hotel? Have we entered into His presence with a "check-in" to "check-out" mentality? Or are we furnishing his home within us so that He might feel comfortable to abide with us? Are we only interested in a quick overnight visitation? Or are we building, day by the day, a foundation necessary for God to live in us as we dwell in him?

No matter who we are or where we are from, something inside of us recognizes the presence of the almighty God. Even carnal people realize "God presence" because He is unavoidable. Romans 1:20 attests to this truth, "for since the creation of the world God's invisible qualities—his eternal power and divine nature—have been clearly seen, being understood from what has been made, so that people are without excuse." These things are in plain sight. The miracle of a newborn, the curing of terminal illnesses, the invention of electricity, the galaxies and the millions of stars that occupy them. All of this is clearly seen. There's no avoiding God in your life. He's too big to ignore. And yet, in our understanding of praise, we have made God so small. We have condescended him to a platform-for-profit, when he wants deeper relationship. We would rather a convenient quickie over a consecrated and concentrated devotional time with him. As we build a house of praise, we must first be honest about the furniture that we have brought into that house that doesn't belong. As we remove the unnecessary, God can replenish us with the essentials.

One of the essentials is the presence of God. It is important for us as people of God to make a commitment to always create an environment where it is unmistakably identified and acknowledged as the place where God dwells. Notice, this commitment is not only for those who lead worship in public spaces on Sunday, but also for everyone who identifies as a disciple of Jesus Christ. Whether in our cars, or on our jobs, wherever it is—the presence of God must be pure and real. The presence of God must be fresh in your heart and spirit. If the leaders in the Lord's church do not consistently focus on building the Lord a house of praise, then we will inevitably play

Russian roulette with the souls who come to the house of God for an encounter with God. If the people in the pews depend on the leaders in the pulpit to cultivate their relationship with God, we will create mini idols of co-dependency, and God will not share his glory with another. Each person—you, your children, your leaders and me must insist on making praise a daily habit of choice. Otherwise, those who come to the well to drink will leave thirsty. Those who come hungry will not have the sustenance necessary to be filled.

In Psalm 66, David encourages his listeners to make a joyful shout to God. But this shout isn't designated for a certain group. The shout must be lifted throughout all the earth. In other words, everyone qualifies. Everyone is expected to shout and sing out of honor of his name. When praise becomes a "Simon says" activity, we miss the point of the encounter. When we place more emphasis on the good singers over the "joyful noise" group, we miss the point of the encounter. There is a sound that is released from heaven when everyone, corporately, gets on one accord to shout unto God. There are certain miracles that will only manifest when we all, together, in one mind, with one spirit, join the heavenly hosts and shout together with one singular goal to kiss heaven with our praise. David says to make his praise glorious. How do we do that –by deliberately and intentionally giving up our right to praise ourselves.

The house of praise is built when we give God what we want to keep for ourselves. The house of praise is built when we humble ourselves in his presence, and remind ourselves that we are absolutely nothing without him. The only way to honor his name is to remove ours from the spotlight. The only way that God will be glorious is if we refuse to accept that which belongs to him. This is why daily declarations are so important to the maintenance of God's fresh presence. Declaring, like David, that God's works are awesome, and that his power is great, puts so much into perspective. Very often, when we do not live a lifestyle of praise, we will give other things priority in our lives because we will focus on those things more than we focus on God. Our finances can rob us of focused praise. Our love life can rob us of focused praise. But the scriptures show us in this psalm that by simply declaring God's great works, and by simply reminding yourself of his power, God will cause your enemies to submit themselves to you. This is the daily commitment of the Praiser.

Whether you know it or not, your praise has power and authority.

Whether you know it or not, your praise has power and authority. When done correctly, it will set the course for your life, for your children, for your family and for whatever the place you find yourself in at the time. Praise is a demonstration. It is an act of your will. Praise is a response to the assurance of who God is in our lives. It is also an act of obedience to GOD since he has commanded all living creatures to praise and celebrate Him without delay. This means, it's not optional. The call must be answered because God has established his children in the earth to respond. So, if praise is an act of your will and a demonstration of your body (including your voice, hands, legs or feet), then worship is an internal response within the soul. Praise is the house, and worship is the furniture. Together, in fellowship with God, we experience a sacred encounter. That encounter is most evident when your heart, soul and mind come face to face with the bigness of who GOD is. Somehow, you become so overwhelmed by his magnitude that the temporary world seems to explode for just a moment as you launch into a majestic encounter with your King. In response to this indescribable moment, some may extend their hands. Others may rock from side to side. Still others may lay prostrate or cry with a loud voice. Either way, it is impossible to experience the power of God and not have a visible response to it. Something within you stands up. Your emotions bow down in reverence to the realization of His power. Your mind surrenders its noisy distractions for a moment—and you are fully present with God, surrounded by His glory.

That is where we want to live. Our aim, through these chapters, is to rebuild the walls that have been torn down in our hearts so we can guard our worship space. Praise is the realization of God's faithfulness. Praise is the resume of experiences that God has proven over time. Worship is when GOD responds to the praise and celebration offerings we send to Him, and gives us permission to go deeper into a fuller and greater GLORY OF HIS PRESENCE. This is the place where God releases clarity in the things of GOD for every area of your life. This is the place where life seems to be bigger than the petty issues around you. This is the place, above the clouds, where turmoil cannot enter; where distractions must wait; where the enemy cannot cloud your mind. The more often you allow yourself to be in His presence, the more inclined your ear will be to the sound of God. And the more your ear is inclined to the sound of God, the easier it will be to recognize a counterfeit spirit.

By building a house of praise, you will become more sensitive to the aroma of His glorious grace and power. By building a house of praise, you will learn the power of unity and relationships. By building a house of praise, you will learn how to declare the Scriptures until strength consumes every weakness. Your praise and worship to GOD gives you access to the Heavenly realm. Don't abuse it. Don't misuse it. Build it.

CHAPTER TWO
Experiencing Pure Worship:
Defining Worship

Create in me a clean heart, O God; and renew a right spirit within me. (Psalm 51:10)

If I were to enlist in the United States Army (highly unlikely at this point, but just go with me ☺) I must endure something called basic training. I may know how to fight, but I still need basic training. I may know how to shoot a gun, but just because I have the ability does not mean that I am ready for battle.

The goal of basic training is designed to be highly intense and extremely challenging. It is a nine-week intensive that insists on stretching you to your limit. You must wake up early. Your diet has to change. You exercise a lot, and your habits will be challenged. All of this is required in the United States Army before any soldier can dare to fight for his or her country on the frontline.

How interesting is it that worship leaders and pastors all around the world are coming to the frontline every Sunday to lead people into His presence, and yet, they have not had basic training. Yes, they may be gifted or have the skillset. Yes, they may be called. But just because you have an instrument doesn't mean it is tuned. In the same way, it is absolutely essential that every person who identifies as a worshipper endure some form of basic training. Especially those who stand in front of us each week to lead us into the great mystery of God's presence; without training, you will certainly derail the people. Without training, you may get the job done, but it will not be done in excellence.

In this chapter, I want to give you Worship 101 basics. I know that many of our worship leaders today walk around with an arrogant disposition as if they do not need to rehearse the basic fundamentals of their craft, but skilled people are skilled because they have consistently rehearsed the basics.

Let me begin by telling you what worship is, and what worship is not. Sure, we hear this word a lot in our churches, but many people can utter the same word and mean something altogether different. To some, worship means to "sing." For others, worship means to roll on the floor until you are foaming at the mouth. Onlookers may call that "crazy" but trust me, somebody reading this might call it worship.

So let's clear the air and start on the same page. Worship is not a list of rules or a bunch of acrobatics that we do in church to elicit a mystical or magical response from heaven. Worship is not a song you sing, but an offering you bring. And when the offering is lifted to God, then the sound of worship ebbs and flows into the heavens. Worship can be demonstrated in many different ways. Some worship through prayer, which is effective communication with God. Prayer establishes an undeniable relationship between you and Your Maker. Others may worship by lifting their hearts to the Lord, or by "groaning or uttering" sounds and poetic verses as a sign of love and compassion to God. Either way, worship requires a heart connection, and where there is no connection, worship ceases to exist.

When we worship, we pay divine honor to God. If you've ever seen a politician walk in a room, even if he is not in his own country, the people usually stand or give an ovation as a sign of honor. If you've ever sat in a courtroom, when the judge enters in, someone will say, "all rise" as a sign of honor. Worship is an honorable endeavor. By honor, I mean we must always realize that we are not on God's level. We are never equal with God. God is not our buddy or our significant other. He is the Lord of Hosts. He is the President of Presidents, and the Commander-in-Chief of Creation. Without honor, worship ceases to exist. Without honor, we lose the value of worship.

Without honor, worship ceases to exist. Without honor, we lose the value of worship.

When we worship correctly, we ascribe honor, dignity and worth to our Maker. In the Hebrew, worship is translated shachah, which means to lower one's body or to stretch out with one's face to the ground as a means of paying honor. This form of reverence is seen a lot in the Old Testament, and especially in temple worship. In the Greek, worship is translated proskuneo, which means to kiss (as a dog would lick his masters hand). I love this definition because it reminds me that worship requires touch. It is impossible to worship God without touching God. In order for worship to be worship, there must be an exchange. There must be contact. God is a spirit, so we do not contact him physically. We contact him spiritually. This is why Jesus said, "those who worship me must worship in spirit and in truth." To worship "in truth" means there are no divides or hidden agendas. In fact, it means there is an unveiled communication with creation and Creator.

Having said that, let me pause to ask this: how can the worship leader encourage others to touch God if he or she hasn't touched God themselves? How can we introduce the lost to Christ if we are strangers in his presence? If we do not honor Him enough to put the phone down, silence the social media noise, and seek His face, then we are not equipped or prepared to lead others to a God that we do not know.

To worship God's way means to throw away the "bling" and bring him blood.

Worship requires touch. Worship requires contact. Most times, when worship was mentioned in the Old Testament, it was always connected to an offering. The first murder in the history of mankind happened because of worship. Cain killed his brother Abel because God accepted one offering and did not accept another.

From the beginning of time, the enemy has fought to destroy worship. When we view worship as an offering, if requires something pure from us. It requires something sacrificial of us. Just giving God the leftovers isn't worship. Just giving God the residue of our concentration isn't worship. In order to worship God's way, we must give him our first-fruits. That means, the beginning of our day; the first from our salary. He must have priority over our relationships, our career goals, our future dreams. God wants it all.

To worship God's way means to throw away the "bling" and to bring him blood. Worship in the Old Testament was a bloody occasion. Animals were sacrificed to God and not just any animal; but only those that were pure enough to be accepted. I'm afraid, in this day that we've lost the art of sacrifice. We've lost the conviction of surrender. We expect immediate elevation without intimate consecration. But when we worship God's way, we empty ourselves in private so He can minister through us in public. Worship is the soul's surrender of will and heart. It cannot be achieved in a rush. God doesn't want a quickie encounter. He wants intimate time; focused attention and our whole being. This is why David said, " bless the Lord oh my soul and all that is within me." God's will for worship involves all that is within you. If we are not willing to give all, then God is not obligated to accept our offering.

Worship cannot be manufactured or generated. In order for worship to exist, all focus must be completely on God. I like to say it this way: praise builds the house, and worship is God moving in. Praise is something we do, and worship is something God releases. We enter into his courts with praise, but it is up to God to respond. His response depends on a few things. How pure is your worship? How clean is your spirit? Is your sound recognizable in the heavens? Does something shift in the spirit realm when the angels see your life? These are all questions that every worshipper should examine and answer honestly.

Bishop Darryl Brister defines worship in this way. He says, "Worship is the air that is breathed through the lungs of faith. It is the oxygen to the brain of the soul. And if you ever refuse to praise and worship God, you will literally die of a suffocated spirit because God desires your praise." This is the heart of worship, friends. Worship is being with God spirit-to-Spirit. Worship is the height of spiritual intimacy. But most importantly, worship requires a heart connection. If we are not connected to God through our worship, then we just may hear the same words Jesus uttered in Matthew, "they worship me with their lips but their hearts are far from me."

NO HEART, NO HONOR

The heart is the most important organ within the anatomy of worship. If there is no heart, then there can be no honor. If there is no honor, then there can be no honesty with God. And yet, the irony of our day is that we have instructors helping us to sing better, to look better, to perform better, but very few leaders are challenging us to deal with our hearts. If we sing without heart, it profits us nothing. If we dance, preach, or teach without heart, it profits us nothing. Real worship is a heart thing.

David's verb choice in Psalm 51 is really important. He could've said, "Give me a clean heart," or "clean the heart I have," but he asked the Lord to **create** a clean heart within him. To create means to **"design"** or to **make;** or to put in me something that wasn't there before. The same way that God created mankind into existence with his hands, David is asking for his clean heart to be created. He knows that the current state of his heart is not pure enough. His heart is not in worship-ready condition. And the only way purity can happen is if God creates it. The only way David can be set in the right direction is if God starts from scratch in his heart.

Notice this closely. David wasn't asking for a pacemaker. He was asking for a transplant. I think that is what our worship is missing in the Lord's church. We want God to take our carnality and give us a pacemaker so that we can experience His presence without changing our lives. But in order for our worship to ascend to God, he's got to start from scratch. We must be willing for him to create in us the thing he wants to do through us. Until the residue disappears from our hearts, we will continue to carry that residue into the house of God. As a result, there will be no signs, wonders, miracles, or long-lasting change. There may be a gust of emotional hype, but only a true encounter with the heart of God's glory will bring real transformation.

So how do we start the process of connecting to God with our hearts? There are many ingredients, but the three most essential to worship are consecration, confession, and intimacy. To be consecrated before God means that you are willing to get your spirit in shape. Romans 12:2 tells us how: "be transformed by the renewing of our minds." In other words, we must offer our lives as living sacrifices. These words are very "churchy" nowadays, but if we put this scripture in the context of old testament sacrifice, it may become clear how difficult this task really is. During the Old Covenant, lambs and doves were slaughtered and offered up to God in order to atone for sin. This required blood. This required killing. This was messy business. To be God's "living sacrifice" means we have to be willing to kill ourselves and endure the bloodiness of our mess, but still live to tell others "for God I live, and for God I will die." This isn't just a ritual practice that happens once a year. This is a practice that must happen every day. Consecration is not a word we can pull out on January 1st when the church goes on a fast. Consecration is a daily decision to self-deny. It is a daily decision to renew our minds in the water of His Word. If we are not actively committed to reading His word, we will not be prepared to die daily to our carnal desires and live anyway.

Confession allows us to be clean and honest with God. Without confession, there is no trust between you and Your creator. Think about it. We only tell the truth of our weaknesses to people we trust. If you are not able to tell God the truth, then you don't trust Him. There is no real relationship established between you and God. This is why John 1:9 says, "If we confess our sins, He is faithful and just to forgive." Proverbs 28:13 goes on to say "the man that hides sin cannot prosper." And all throughout Psalms 51, David is open and honest about the dark, dirty, and nasty parts of his life. The reality is, there is nothing we can say, be , or do that can catch God off guard. He is our maker and knows everything about us. Intimacy is running the risk of exposing the wrinkles, bulges and scars and never having it thrown back in your face. And that is what GOD wants from us: *intimacy*.

Ask yourself: how much do you really confess to God? Do you tell your friends more than you tell your God? Do you run to counselors or professionals quicker than you run to your secret place? If you had to rate your level of transparency with God, how would you score? The ironic thing about God is that we cannot hide from him; yet he allows us to confess our sins to Him as a sign of relationship and co-dependency.

Finally, a heart connection with God depends on intimacy. Return to the definition of proskuneo. As a dog licking his master's hand, or running to greet him at the door, our intimacy with God must be palpable. We must touch him with our song. We must touch him with our words. We must touch him with our lives. If we sing, talk, and live without touching God, we have offered up nothing more than sounding brass and tinkling cymbals. How do we develop intimacy? By rising up early to seek Him (Psalm 63). By longing for him more than we long for human affection (Psalm 42). By accepting that we will have to endure seasons of suffering in order to truly know him intimately (Philippians 3:10). These are all ways to *know* him.

That word "know" in the Old Testament is translated to mean intercourse with, or sexual intimacy between. When Adam *knew* Eve, they had a child and named him Cain. When Abraham *knew* Sarah, they conceived Isaac. When we *know* God intimately, worship is conceived. The only way worship can be birthed into the earth is through our knowing him. The only way worship can be released in our churches is through intimacy with the Father. This is where after we court God the Father through our Lord Jesus Christ we develop an intimate relationship with him. Then in fellowship with Him, He releases His anointing into our spiritual wombs where he impregnates us with our purpose and His Apostolic Anointing and Destiny. One thing we must be mindful of is that GOD will not two-time us or do a back seat deal with us. He, in fact, wants to be the lover of our souls. He will not share us with another god. His expectation is to be all and everything.

Over the next few weeks, take inventory of your heart connection with God. How consecrated is your life? How committed are you to daily confession and prayer? Are you intimate with your Maker, or just familiar with Him? If you desire a stronger connection with God, it will not begin with your skill. It will only start with the heart.

CHAPTER THREE
The Danger of Worshipping Worship

"The earth is the Lord's, and the fulness thereof; the world, and they that dwell therein. For he hath founded it upon the seas, and established it upon the floods. Who shall ascend into the hill of the Lord? or who shall stand in his holy place? He that hath clean hands, and a pure heart; who hath not lifted up his soul unto vanity, nor sworn deceitfully. He shall receive the blessing from the Lord, and righteousness from the God of his salvation." (Psalm 24:1-5)

Worship is a word that will never go out of style. How do I know? Because everybody worships something. Whether you worship the true and living God, or you worship the house you live in, you worship something. You may not worship a material possession, but you may struggle with worshipping a person, or a position. "Worship," simply defined, means to ascribe worth to; to honor something above all else because it is the primary object of your affection and attention. It's the thing you go to first. It's the person you wake up thinking about. It's the career you will do anything to secure. It's the body you work hard to get. It's the love or the touch that you can never get enough of. Everybody—
Christian, Atheist, Muslim, or monk, worships something. But the problem I see in our 21st Century Churches is that we have become worshippers of worship. We have become more in love with the sight and sound of

"church" that we have lost the sanctity and sacredness of Christ. We have removed Christ as the center of our lives, and we invite him in as the guest preacher when something goes wrong. This epidemic that is sweeping through our churches is far more dangerous than Ebola, anthrax, or any of these overnight viruses.

Simply put, Jesus must remain the center of it all. Our tendency to worship worship results in a false experience of high energy and entertainment that we mistake for a true-God encounter. When we worship worship, we care more about the personality in front of us than the God above us. When we worship worship, we can't sing unless the microphones are perfectly balanced, and the people are standing with their hands lifted. When we worship worship, we run toward the image of high church, concert church, or website-ready church, and the problem is, God can't figure out the last time you were in his presence without the pomp and circumstance. My question to every worship leader and public voice reading this chapter is simple: are you guilty of worshipping worship?

Psalm 24:1-5 is one of my absolute favorite passages to quote during the exhortation moment in corporate worship. It reminds us that the earth is God's and we are only able to enter into his holy place if our hands are clean and our hearts are pure. I know this isn't very popular nowadays to preach or to teach, but our offerings will not be accepted until our hearts are pure and our hands are clean. Consider the Message version of this same passage. I love the way the writer puts it: "God claims Earth and everything in it, God claims World and all who live on it. He built it on Ocean foundations, laid it out on River girders. Who can climb Mount God? Who can scale the holy north-face? Only the clean-handed, only the pure-hearted; Men who won't cheat, women who won't seduce. God is at their side; with God's help they make it."

There's no way around it. In order to "climb Mount God" we must be willing to sacrifice the idols of skill, stage, stuff, status, and sensation. These are some of the ways that we worship worship. As I said earlier in this chapter, the problem in the Lord's church is that we have gone from worshiping the King, to worshiping worship. We've gotten to a place where we celebrate worship and use it as a banner for our own glory, but God's throne will not be shared with another (no matter how famous, important, or talented we are). Our problem is, we glory in the fact that we have the ability to get into a place where we sense God and we know that people react to our gift (you know, they get goose bumps when you sing and all of that), but worship is not a feeling, worship is a filling. When God responds to our praise, he fills our well with fresh water. If there is no filling, then there is no encounter. All we have done is offered up noise and sweated out of our clothes.

This is why it is so important that every worship pastor and every apostolic leader is willing to sound an alarm to us as believers until we are able to bring integrity back to the house of God. Simply put, Jesus must remain the center of it all. We should not be focusing on our ability to orchestrate a gathering, but on our ability to bring back the purity of God's heart so that the people of God can have an encounter with God. Remember, worship only becomes worship when God responds to the purity of our praise. It's not about the top 20 songs that we sing. It's not about having a great instrument or a great voice. What's interfering with our access into the majesty of his power is our tendency to prize gifts and skills over God and sanctification.

We worship others' skill. We want to be like those

who "look the part." We worship by our feelings alone. We look for sensation and emotion, and so we only think God has manifested himself when we are crying or running around the church. We lust for the stage. If we aren't on it, we won't open our mouths or lift our hands. The stage is our goal, not the holy of holies. We want to be seen, noticed, appreciated, compensated, validated, and all of that is fine in its place, but when your focus becomes *that* over *Him*, you are worshipping worship. We look for the stuff—you know, the money, the materials, and the momentary high—to supply us with that which only God can give. We worship our celebrity status and God is standing on the sideline, waiting for us to call Him into the encounter that has His name on it. He's calling us to represent Him with more integrity. We are not called to the altar of God's sanctuary to be platform hoards. We are not called to the altar of God's sanctuary to be popular and significant. What he has called us to is sacrifice. You know, like getting up at 5 in the morning to worship. He's calling us to sacrifice so that we can shake ourselves from the inebriation of our own abilities. God wants our hearts. He's unimpressed with our gifts. He wants to know if He can call us friend and servant, and whether or not He can depend on us to represent Him.

Psalm 66 says to "make a joyful noise unto God, all ye lands: Sing forth the honour of his name: make his praise glorious." The reality is, God is calling us to make His praise glorious. Outside of the platform, in our families, in our neighborhoods, in the grocery stores—we are called to make His praise glorious. How do we do that? By extending some small act of love and kindness into the world so people will notice the God in us and not us. When is the last time you sowed a seed and didn't write your name on the envelope? When is the last time you blessed someone but didn't tell anyone? When is the last time you visited a loved one in the hospital and sang them into the glory of the Lord? Without the cameras, or the instagram pictures, or the attention from the crowd, when is the last time you shut down your schedule just to spend some quality time with the Lord?

In the Old Testament, the Levites wore something called an ephod. The purpose of the ephod was not just to be in uniform, but to hide the flesh so that no flesh could be identified. In our churches today, we are becoming more like the world because we want to be accepted. We want to be seen. We want to be complimented. We want to get all of the attention. But God is challenging us to be a called out people who have the mark of holiness. I'm not talking about a white skirt or a cross on our chests. More specifically, I'm talking about a cross on our lives, where people can hear the sound of God's voice through us. Where is your modern day ephod? How do we know that you are a Levite? What does your life say when your song stops? What

He wants to know if He can call us friend and servant, and whether or not He can depend on us to represent Him.

does your heart reveal when somebody else gets the opportunity you've always wanted? I think our churches need a worship exam. We need to pay close attention to what the crowd says after you have ministered. In my opinion, one of the most offensive things in the world is when people say to me, "I love it when you sang that song... You took me to that place." To me, this means that I didn't do my assignment correctly because at the end of the day, I don't want you to hear my voice. I don't want to distract you from His presence. I want you to hear God speak to your heart. And if I never sing, I want the sound of His voice to arrest the environment and pull you closer to His heart.

Did you know that it is possible to have worship without ever singing a song? Zephaniah 3:17 says, "The Lord thy God in the midst of thee is mighty; he will save, he will rejoice over thee with joy; he will rest in his love, he will joy over thee with singing." The ultimate goal of the worship leader is not to "take the people in" or to "get the attention so that you can get invited back." Instead, our primary goal is to be so connected to the Master that the songs we sing are not ours, but the ones He sings through us. Our primary goal is to become invisible, so that God might beckon His people to come to where He is. If we are going to change this epidemic of worshipping worship, then we need to get out of the way. We must stop taking his platform and using it for our purposes. We must stop stealing God's shine. Our only job is to make His praise glorious. It's in Him that we live and move and have our being. To keep ourselves in check, we should ask the Lord every day, "How do You want me to set this platform? How do You want me to move? What do You want me to say to Your people? What is Your plan today to help them experience You?" You'd be surprised how many worship teams will sing to people without ever praying to their God. You'd be surprised how many rehearsals are conducted in the house of God without lifting up a special song, or a scripture, or a devotional in thanks to God. These are symptoms of a much larger issue. In my opinion, the Lord's church is in a state of emergency. We are using His platform to audition for things that have nothing to do with Him. We want a popular album and we want people to like us and invite us to their concerts. But the integrity of our heart is in question. We need to come to the place of truth and realize that we are nothing without the Lord. The charisma that causes people to like us is not the anointing that will sustain us. The only way God will anoint us for the assignment is when He sees us in his presence after the assignment. It is important for us to get to a place where we just want to serve the King. So wherever the cloud of the glory of God is moving, we move with the cloud and not with what's popular.

The reality is, we're not always going to hit the mark, but that's the purpose of grace. We won't always stand before God's people and have our hearts completely clear of the clutter from this world, but that doesn't mean we shouldn't work toward maturing in our Christian discipleship. Thankfully, God, who knows how wretched and trifling we can be, enables us with His grace to do what we are not able to do on our own. But what's happening in our churches is that we are trying to function without His grace. We are trying to function as his grace, not with his grace. We are trying to occupy a role that he didn't call us to. Again, I remind you: the Psalmist asks, "Who shall ascend the hill of the LORD? Who shall stand in His holy place? He or she who has clean hands and a pure heart." The Message version says, he who has not "seduced." Think about that for a second. When we worship worship, we are subtly seducing people into a place of dishonor. When they honor us instead of honoring God, we become the mini-idol standing between God and the people. We become the mistress that the church is cheating on God with. There must be a place where we place God at the altar of every situation, and in order to keep him there, we've got to get out of the way.

We need to get to a place where God embraces us with His love and we have a new encounter with Him so that He can trust us again to use us to make a difference in the lives and hearts of His people. We need to make a difference not just on the platform, but even when there's no worship team. That way, when we lift up our voices and sing the praises of our King, Heaven responds to it.

I encourage all of us to make His praise glorious. Let's divorce ourselves from our insatiable desire to be validated by people. There is a difference between charisma and anointing. Charisma will cause people to follow you, but the anointing of God will cause people to go straight to where your God is and say yes to Him. When we worship worship, nothing happens. But when we worship God, nothing can remain the same.

CHAPTER FOUR
Spiritual Hygiene

The earth is the Lord's, and everything in it, the world, and all who live in it; for he founded it on the seas and established it on the waters. Who may ascend the mountain of the Lord? Who may stand in his holy place? The one who has clean hands and a pure heart, who does not trust in an idol or swear by a false god. They will receive blessing from the Lord and vindication from God their Savior. (Psalm 24:1-5)

In June 2014, after my dad celebrated his 70th birthday, he was diagnosed with cancer. It was a nerve-wrecking experience. Hundreds of questions came to mind, but my only desire was to relieve him from his pain.

As we sat in the examination room, the nurse came in to take his vital signs. I noticed a sign on the wall that read, "All health care professionals must wash their hands before attending to patients," signed by Hospital Management. As the nurse moved around in the room, she apparently had no intention of obeying the sign. She sneezed two or three times and we said, "God Bless You," but then, we watched her proceed, without blinking or thinking, toward my father to take his vitals! At that very moment, I said to her in a very stern voice, "Before you touch my father, I'm going to need you to wash your hands." She told me that she hadn't sneezed in her hands and he would be fine. She was defensive and I was trying to be protective. My father wasn't feeling the best, and I didn't want to make him more upset. So I calmed down and made a mental note to myself: *before you touch my father, I'm going to need you to wash your hands.*

All of us have experienced it before. If it's not a nurse in a hospital, it's an employee at a restaurant. All of us have gone into a public bathroom and bumped into someone who didn't wash his hands. I don't know how you feel about it, but it absolutely disgusts me to know that people don't care enough about their personal hygiene to wash their hands after they have used the bathroom. But even worse than people not caring about themselves, is when you see an employee do the same. When employees, especially those who work in restaurants, do not wash their hands in front of me, I am determined to leave the premises immediately. Why? Because they are leaders in that corporate space, and their lack of hygiene could affect my health or the health of those I love.

The same is true for the worship leader. It's one thing for lay members to enter into his presence with dirty hands. It's another thing for you to do the same. When leaders and Levites are not concerned about their spiritual hygiene, they can infect and contaminate the atmosphere without even knowing it. We are leaders, and as such, there is a high premium of responsibility placed upon those who usher in the presence of the Lord. For this reason, our hands must be clean, our hearts must be pure, our minds must be renewed, and our souls must be converted. Before we go further, I just want to know: how is your hygiene? How often do you wash yourself in the presence of the Lord?

Everywhere I go, the Lord urges me to remind leaders of the importance of spiritual hygiene. And by spiritual hygiene, I mean the importance of daily washing, soaking, and bathing in the presence of the Lord. Have you ever been around someone who did not wash? Have you ever rushed out of the house and smelled the must emanating from your armpits? Well, imagine what it must be like to go weeks without washing? Imagine if you only washed one time per week. Even though you took a shower on Sunday, it doesn't mean you will not smell and reek with odor by Wednesday. No matter how much cologne you try to put on to hide it, there is an odor that dirty bodies just can't hide. There is a smell that can't be squelched by a little soap and water. In order to clean your body, you have to rinse thoroughly and daily.

I know this seems like a simple lesson but you'd be surprised by how many worship leaders only dip in the water of his presence on Sunday morning. And then, by the middle of the week, they try to sprinkle a little cologne on to cover their odor, but their flesh has been reeking of disobedience and sin all week long. If you are not prepared to soak in his presence on a daily basis, then you are not deserving of the platform to lead. Our responsibility as worship leaders is to help the congregation see the full picture of what worship is: all the shapes, colors and sounds of which it is composed. If the picture of worship is going to have depth and variety, then we have to paint with different brushes. We have to familiarize ourselves with the various paint strokes necessary to present different images. Our approach to worship, then, has to be deliberate. It must always be about God. We must always start with a clean canvas. It must never be about you, your skillset or your voice. It's about being grateful that God would use

> When leaders and Levites are not concerned about their spiritual hygiene, they can infect and contaminate the atmosphere without even knowing it.

you to impact the community of believers that you're responsible for—and my friends, if you are not clean in your spirit you will never be empty of your flesh.

You have to paint with different brushes. Everything can't be what you like or what you want to happen. Psalm 66:2 says, "Make a joyful noise unto God, all ye lands: Sing forth the honour of his name: make his praise glorious." The key responsibility of every worship leader is not to get validation from the congregation on how great your voice is or how charismatic you are. Charisma can never replace anointing. Anointing is God's validation of you that He's equipped you and prepared you to be used. But at the same time, the anointing doesn't give you license to be arrogant or narcissistic. It doesn't make you an exception, but makes you responsible for creating an environment that God can speak and move in.

I have seen so many anointed people be dirtied by an egotistical personality and a narcissistic spirit. They become as self-righteous as the Pharisees in Jesus' day, and they think that by drawing a line in the sand between the holy and the unholy, that God is pleased with their sacrifice. But this, my friends, is just as problematic as the singer who clubs all night on Saturday, and then shows up on Sunday to offer her sound to the Lord. Both are filthy in God's presence. Your attitude will determine your altitude. And your discipline will affect your destiny. How you live before men will exalt you in due season. A heart set on being clean in the presence of the Lord will not always make every decision according to God's will, but they will linger in the presence of the Lord in private, so that God can sing through, play through, dance through, and preach through them in public.

...the anointing doesn't give you license to be arrogant or narcissistic.

Which leads me to my next observation. I believe that there's some confusion in our churches today as it relates to the intersection of ministry and industry. It must be said and it must be taught from storefront to mega-church. Ministry and industry are not related. The responsibility of ministry is to help people experience the manifest presence of a real God. Charisma will cause people to like you, but the anointing will cause people to trust the God mantle in you. Charisma will cause people to notice you and to follow you. But the anointing will help people to be guided by you to where God is.

What's happening in our churches today is that we are releasing responsibility to people who have not spent time with God. Paul says, "I want to know Him in the power of His resurrection." But how do you get to know God? By fellowshipping with Him and spending time with Him. You'd be surprised by how many artists are popular with people but strangers to God. You'd be surprised by how many singers only sing a song to Jesus during worship rehearsal and on Sunday morning. Psalm 24:3-4 says, "Who shall ascend into the hill of the LORD? Or who shall stand in his holy place? He that hath clean hands, and a pure heart; who hath not lifted up his soul unto vanity." Today, we have unfortunately become an idolatrous generation. We are obsessed with people validating us until God stands on the sidelines and watches us get the praise. And because there's always someone crying out to God, He will always find a way to bring release to the people in the congregation. But that isn't license to live how we want to live and play how we want to play. God's glory will remain in the house when our spirits are cleansed daily by the Word.

Our churches stand in need of a spiritual cleanse. And the more I travel and the more I observe, the more I realize what is happening today. Quite simply, we are forfeiting our private worship for the privilege to have leadership in corporate worship. But this is completely twisted and erroneous because what God does in private worship, He will not do in corporate worship. Your private worship is naked, scarred, wrinkled and unashamed. In private worship, God says, "Come close to Me. I know you're nasty. I know you lie. I know you cheat. But come close to Me because I want to show you who I've called you to be." This is how you are cleansed in private by practicing the presence of the LORD. It's spiritual hygiene, God's way. If you do not wash yourself in the presence of the LORD, you will not have the validation or the apostolic authority to stand on a platform and tread through the waters to help people to experience God. But instead of us being cleansed in private, we end up bleeding in public. We end up turning exhortation into exploitation. And the time that should be shared in worship with others, is now a time in which the worship leader is getting private surgery in a public service. I know you've witnessed it before. The worship leader begins to weep uncontrollably and it's clear that God is working on them personally. But because no one has taught him or her the correct way to go before God, we turn this public act of surgery into the new trend to evoke a response from the people. But this is not what God wants. He doesn't want us bleeding onto the congregation. When we are cleansed in his presence in private, he deals with our stuff at home; so that we can usher others into that very presence in church.

If that isn't happening in church, then we are trying to steal a consecrated moment in order to turn it into a celebrity moment. In other words, we try to steal the spotlight from God by doing runs, tricks, and riffs to garner the attention from the crowd. But this isn't pleasing in God's sight either. Therefore, I challenge worship leaders to stop being praise hordes where people have to celebrate you. Settle yourself and know that if God calls you, then He will open doors for you. Because God loves you, He will also chase you. He may even send people into your life to correct you so that you can learn balance. Far too many leaders are looking for validation in a place where God's glory is the only thing deserving of attention. Ever since Lucifer was excommunicated from heaven, there's been a contest for position. We always want to be validated and approved. But my challenge to you is to stay in the Word of God. If you stay in His Word, then there's no reason for you to look for validation. God will raise up people who will thank you for helping them experience His voice.

APPROACH YOUR ASSIGNMENT DELIBERATELY

We have to be very deliberate in how we approach our assignments. In Ezekiel 44:5 God says, "mark well, and behold with thine eyes, and hear with thine ears all that I say unto thee concerning all the ordinances of the house of the LORD." Quite simply, we have a sacred mandate from a Holy God. There are demons on assignment who are trying to suffocate the glory of God's presence. Our assignment as worship pastors is not to sing the top 20 songs of the week, but to provoke God's response. Remember: it only becomes worship if He responds to it; if we allow it to come from the purest place of our hearts. That's when it becomes worship. And when we offer up a pure and holy sacrifice worthy of his response, then God will have the final say so in the corporate encounter.

I believe that if we get spiritual hygiene right, then we will see signs, miracles, and healing happening in the church again. I believe that we're living in a time where God is raising the sound of the kingdom all over the world. I call it the Master Plan. He's strategically orchestrating, in every denomination and race, a way for us to understand what His heart's desire is. When the earth is over as we know it, there will be no more sermons preached, but what we will do forever is praise Him and honor Him for the rest of eternity. So He's teaching all of us how to honor Him and sing His songs and stroke His presence. For that reason, this gift we know as worship cannot be about us. It can't be about our personal need for validation. When we make worship about us, we move into a place of witchcraft and idolatry. But God will not share His glory with another god, whether it's a strange god around you or you yourself!

...it only becomes worship if He responds to it.

Let me put something parenthetically here. The new strange god in our pulpits is the cell phone. We can't focus on worship because we're so busy trying to catch the moment that we miss the moment! We're so busy trying to capture the presence so we can post it on facebook, that we miss the presence in the process. Receive this in love, friends. God is not to be displayed as a new production of reality TV. There's got to be a place where we consecrate the moment of true worship. That's why we have media people—their responsibility is to capture the moment. Your responsibility is to gravitate to the sound and the wind of God's presence.

We cannot play with people's lives. We are required to take the bloodstained lives of these people and give them the blood of Jesus. You have been entrusted to deliver to them something that sounds like, feels like and tastes like Heaven. When Jesus teaches the disciples how to pray, He tells them to pray, "Your kingdom come, Your will be done, on Earth as it is in

Heaven." That's one of our responsibilities—to find out what's going on in Heaven and duplicate it here on Earth. When we do what's being done in Heaven, then God will come and take the offering and put His name on it. This is when deliverance comes, restoration comes, hope comes, power comes and people will inevitably receive clarity.

MAKE HIS PRAISE GLORIOUS

It's our responsibility to make His praise glorious. We do this in several ways. We do this by taking the attention off of us. We do it by making sure our attire is appropriate. Anything that you wear that causes people to be distracted is being used by the Devil. You don't know the deacon's struggle or the struggle of anyone else in the room so you need to be mindful of this whenever you dress for worship. We should not be able to see your inner parts. This is not just for the women, but for the men as well. How are you going to wear tightfitting clothes and expect the people to be attracted to God? My friends, we stand in the need of cleansing, and this entire subject of presentation and apparel goes right back to the issue of corporate worship vs. private worship. Private worship is naked, corporate worship is not. If corporate worship is naked, then it becomes perverted. But that's not the nature of our God. Just because it's popular and fashionable does not mean it's consecrated for holiness. I'm not talking about wearing skirts down to your ankles or white stockings. I'm talking about reverencing the opportunity to take the attention off of you. In the Old Testament, whenever the Levites went to minister, they all looked alike. They all wore a sacred garment called the ephod. The purpose of the ephod wasn't to be fashionable, but to take the attention off of them and to put it on the glory of God. I submit to you that we have to go back to that.

Several years ago, the Lord led me to take my worship team out of casual attire for a period and put them in priestly garments. I wanted the congregation to see what sacred postures looked like and to appreciate the reverence connected to it. I wanted them to tune their ears into what the Lord was saying through the preaching and singing through the worship. I don't believe every church should do this, but I do believe that we have to make sure that the praise that we present is designed to make His praise glorious. How we pray, how we prepare our teaching, how we play on the keyboard, all has to point to Him. He wants to be the lover of your soul and the chief and master of it all. Our responsibility is to make His praise glorious.

Ask yourself, "Who shall ascend to the hill of the LORD?" Who can stand in that place? The answer is simple: He who has clean hands and a pure heart, who has not lifted up his soul unto another. Yet we live in a generation that is idolatrous. We find ourselves so easily distracted by things that keep us from hearing God. That's why we don't have power in our services anymore—because we're too busy trying to capture the hottest shouts and the hottest runs. There needs to be someone crying out to prepare the way of the LORD and then we will witness signs and wonders in our services. Nobody will have to lay hands or spit on anybody. All you have to do is create a sound that God responds to and His presence alone will bring healing.

GOD'S PULPIT IS NOT A PLATFORM

Isaiah 10:27 tells us that the anointing of God and the oil of his presence, validates us by lifting burdens and by destroying yokes. It's important for us to understand what our role is. Our posture has to change. Our posture has to be to serve the people of God instead of wanting to be served. We need to host the presence of God.

It grieves me that we're using the platforms that God has entrusted us with to audition for things that aren't even God-focused. That's not the place to let people know you can sing. That platform is to be consecrated as holy to make a difference that will change people's lives forever. It is for God to restore broken families and bring fathers back to their sons and daughters back to their mothers. You can only lead worship through the empowerment of the Holy Spirit because you can't know the inner workings of others' situations. You have to depend on the unction of the Holy Spirit.

Some people will say, "Well, I don't really hear from God." But I say, whenever you find it hard to hear from God, it's because you haven't spent enough time in His presence. When God speaks, He speaks through His Word. Oftentimes we want someone to pray for us or to spit on us. We're so drawn to the fanaticism, but that's not always how God wants to move. He wants to know if you're going to create a space and a time where it's just you and Him so that you can get to know who He really is. So when people get up to say, "God said this.", you'll know if it's really from God. Scripture says, "My sheep know my voice." The reason we don't know His voice is because we're too busy trying to make up time with Him on the platform. But that's not what the platform is for.

2 Timothy 2:15 says that we have to study to show ourselves approved of God. How horrible would it be if our pastors got up on Sunday week after week, and experimented on us, not spending time with God, but just grabbing stuff from the wind, and using the organist to tune up foolishness? We would become a very sick

people. We would become a very depressed people. 2 Timothy 2:20 says that in the house there are vessels of wooden clay and vessels of honor. In other words, you have to choose what you want to be. I want to be used of God. I don't have time to be worried about foolishness. I want God to know that I'm making a difference for His name's sake. Why? Because God is real. God is powerful. He is changing people's lives, He's saving souls and He's setting people free. For this reason, we've got to represent him in a better way than what we're doing. Let's be honest. We're arrogant and we're puffed up. We don't pray for people and help them come to Christ—we talk about them and disparage them when they are down.

Examine yourself by answering this question: When was the last time you led somebody to Jesus? You'd be surprised by how many worship leaders have never evangelized the lost. In their minds, it's not in their job description. In their minds, they think that's the preacher's job. But, I would beg to differ. As a worship leader, you're in a preaching position. You have the responsibility to help people experience God. You are consecrated to be in a priestly position.

These books, seminars and conferences don't mean anything if unbelievers and backsliders don't come to a place of repentance. We dance but we're not happy. We shout but we have no victory. We don't tithe but we expect God to shower down victory. Friends, there are contingencies for the blessings of the Lord that make you rich. I'm not talking about being rich in finances alone. I'm talking about being rich in your calling. I'm talking about being able to access the things of God that make a difference for the people of God. You're not going to know how to flow in the Spirit of God if you have no connection with God. You will get in the pulpit making up stuff and using Gospel clichés, but the people will never encounter God if you don't know the God of the encounter.

THE CHALLENGE

My challenge to you is to find out what's in your hand and in your heart. Look at your role as a leader. Are you making an apostolic difference? Or are you up there playing Russian roulette with people's lives? You don't know what's in the chamber. You can lead people the wrong way and shoot their spiritual head off. It's extremely important that we understand that this is an incredible privilege that God has given us. If you're a worship pastor or a musician and you're not taking any music classes anywhere or any Bible classes and if you don't have a mentor or anything that helps keep the flow going, then you're the great wonder with all the answers—and that isn't good. The reality is, the best worship leaders haven't even taken the platform yet—they're still stumbling around in practice. As soon as you think that you have it all together, God will raise up someone else, fill them with His Spirit, take the sin off of their lives and use them to make a monumental difference in the world.

Our responsibility is to help people to experience who God is. Some people don't feel comfortable raising their hands or singing out loud. We have to teach them how to articulate what's in their hearts. The Scripture says that out of your belly will flow rivers of living water. Hebrews 13:15 says that the sacrifice of praise is the fruit of your lips, which means that there must be an articulation of the glorious presence of God. It's not going to happen through osmosis. We have to grab the truth of God, spend time in His word and ask Him for grace to be able to articulate it to His people so that they can run with it and have an encounter with Him that has nothing to do with our personalities or our egos.

I no longer accept invitations or sing anywhere if I feel that it is unproductive or has no redemptive power. If there's no redemptive power, then we're just sweating and dancing and God's not even there. But every time we get together, something has to happen that causes Heaven to take notice. The Scripture says that God wants to be with us, so our responsibility is to create moments that cause Him to come down from glory to be with us. Whatever the need is, His presence will fulfill it. That's the kind of God we serve. As worship leaders, our responsibility is to drop nuggets everywhere we go to help people experience God. It doesn't have to be deep or spooky, but practical. Paul says, "that I might know Him and the fellowship of His suffering." That I might know Him—His characteristics, His behaviors, the fragrance that makes His presence His presence. My challenge to you, wherever you serve, is to make His praise glorious and to help people experience the presence of God. The only way we can do that in public, is if we clean up in private.

CHAPTER FIVE
Fruit that Remains

I am the true vine, and my Father is the gardener. He cuts off every branch in me that bears no fruit, while every branch that does bear fruit he prunes so that it will be even more fruitful. You are already clean because of the word I have spoken to you. Remain in me, as I also remain in you. No branch can bear fruit by itself; it must remain in the vine. Neither can you bear fruit unless you remain in me.
(John 15:1-4)

The topic of "abiding with God" has been in my spirit for a long time. In all of my experiences as a servant of the Lord's church in the position of worship leader, I've always sensed that God was challenging me to make sure, after I complete an assignment for His glory, that I had made an impact. I've always felt like God was hovering over me, watching me like a teacher peers over his students who are taking an exam, to make sure that I touch the hearts of the people in such a way that healing and deliverance can happen in His presence, for his glory. Making an impact has become a consistent theme when I am asked to teach, because many of us want an experience with God but not an encounter with him. When you experience him, you can go back to how things were because the moment is only an emotional escape. But when you encounter God, you will never be the same.

Like Jacob, you leave his presence with a limp that testifies to the fact that you've been with God. Like Mary, after you encounter God, the womb of your creativity is impregnated with the power of God's glory, and you sense that you can do all things through Christ because His strength becomes realized. An encounter with God is a life-changing, life-altering moment that moves you from the outer courts of wonder into the inner courts of worship. When you make an impact on the lives of God's people, it's not because of your talent or your song; more exactly, it's because of your fruit and because of your heart.

Only those who are surrendered and submitted to God, have the power to make an impact on God's people. Only those who diligently seek him will inherit the reward of his residential presence. By residential presence, I mean that God will remain with you. He won't treat you like a hospital patient—only showing up when you need him. He won't visit you like a hotel guest—only coming to you during moments of transition. But when you remain in His presence, he will reside with you always. Everywhere you go, you carry the emblem of his glory within you. That is the goal—to live a lifestyle of worship such that God's presence, power, and glory will remain with us at all times.

GOD IS THE VINE, WE ARE THE BRANCHES

As "Leaders in the Lords Church," I believe that sometimes we get our signals concerning our assignment mixed up. But the word of the Lord says," I am the vine and you are the branches and without me, you can bear no fruit..." In other words, without My presence, you cannot accomplish anything. Or, another way of saying it is, without My influence, you will never make a lasting impression on the hearts of the people. So, without God, we can't complete the assignment. Without God, we can't concoct, create, or conjure up an atmosphere. And yet, so many worship leaders try to take people to a place of worship without the main ingredient: GOD. This is the never-ending challenge that we, as leaders in the Lord's church, face. It has become an epidemic of disturbing proportions.

So many worship leaders try to take people to a place of worship without the main ingredient: GOD.

Often times, as I travel, I hear and see many great teachers, preachers and singers. I watch people and I try to tune into the "outpour of their hearts." Is this presenter willing to pour out from a heart that will supersede their intellect, education and skillful ability? Is this person willing to deposit more than "a Prepared Presentation"? Will this minister impart a life changing, life giving, love-led nugget of fruit that will outlive their personal visitation? Unfortunately, I'm disturbed and often disappointed because what we are left with is just enough to know how good, how articulate, how educated and how charismatic the presenter is. Often times we, as "leaders in the Lord's Church," leave just enough information that make people in awe of us, not Him.

But what I've learned about real fruit is that even when you have consumed it and even when you have fully digested it, and even when you can no longer see it, there is a lasting impact made in you that is nourishing and impactful to your development. That is what a real leader does—they pour so much of themselves into the moment, that when they have left the scene, generations after them are still flourishing. Real leaders understand that helping people go beyond where we are is our chief responsibility.

I love reading scriptures that say things like, "…. There was a certain man or there were certain woman who…." These scriptures never give us a name, but the verse is so lasting, that even two thousand years later and more than 42 generations later, we are still eating from and being nourished by the lessons from that chapter.

Our church says this every Sunday to our visitors and congregation: "Where God is developing dynamic disciples". And I believe in that motto, but I also believe it needs to go on to say that we are **...after all of the singing has ended, and after all of the preaching has ceased, make sure you are connected to the vine.** developing disciples through our witness and through His word working in our lives. My prayer to God is that I have a lasting impact everywhere I go. I pray often that if people never remember my name and if people never remember the song I sing, or if they never remember what I have on when I'm in front of them, that by the grace of God, they leave there with "fruit that will remain." I'm praying that a seed of hope and a nugget of truth will take root in their hearts and ultimately change their nature so much so that their children's children will be nurtured from that moment of impartation.

A couple of years ago, I was approached by this young lady who asked me, "Do you remember me?" I didn't recall her face, but she continued, "I remember you from when we used to ride the bus together when you were going to Duke Ellington School of the Arts". She went on to say we were on the 30 bus route going up Pennsylvania Avenue and that particular day, she was crying and very upset. She said I asked her if she was alright and I offered to help her. She told me no, and I said that I would love to pray for her. After I prayed, she told me that she had had an abortion and she thought that God would never forgive her. She said she wanted to die, but God used me to tell her that she wouldn't die and that God had already forgiven her. Long story short, she stopped me years later to say, "I am just so glad to see you again. I want you to know that I'm married now and this is my daughter God gave me." And to be perfectly honest, I didn't remember that encounter until she told me.

My challenge to you is simple: after all of the singing has ended, and after all of the preaching has ceased, make sure you are connected to the vine. Make sure that you are focused on bearing much fruit and that you are producing "fruit that remains". The word of Lord says in Luke 3:9, "and even now the ax is laid to the root of the trees. Therefore every tree which does not bear good fruit is cut down and thrown into the fire." John 15:2 goes on to say, "every branch in Me that does not bear fruit He takes away, and every branch that bears fruit he prunes, that it may bear more fruit." Later, in John 15:8, Jesus declares, "This is for my Father's glory, that you bear much fruit, showing yourselves to be my disciples". Verse 16 of that same passage says, "You didn't choose yourself; I chose you and appointed you that you should go and bear fruit and that your fruit should remain so that whatever you ask of the Father, He may give it to you."

FRESH FRUIT

In my humble opinion, too many of us have fruit but lack faithfulness. We are like one-hit wonders, only around until the next gig comes to take us away. But God wants fruit that remains. And not only does he want your faithfulness, but he wants you to be fresh fruit in his presence. When I go to the supermarket I take my time in the produce section because I don't just want any kind of fruit, I want fresh fruit. Have you ever gone to the grocery store to purchase fruit? If you're like me, I will spend twenty minutes poking away at apples and oranges just to make sure that I am buying the freshest fruit available. What a disappointment it is to buy bananas that look good on the outside but are old and spoiled on the inside.

The same is true in God. When He looks down from heaven, He's not just looking for fruit. He's looking for FRESH FRUIT. He's looking for people who are ripe and ready. It is not enough to go to church or sing in the choir. Your fruit has got to be fresh. It's not enough to be involved in your community. You've got to be fresh and attentive so that you attract people to the King.

Have you ever tasted something stale (after having paid good money for it)? The first thing you think is, "that was a waste! I hope I don't get sick from this!" Imagine if God drew those same conclusions about our worship. You see, not only is stale worship "bad tasting," but it can potentially harm your church. Just think about those moments in worship when someone sings the wrong song, or when a talented musician distracts the listener from a true worship moment. Our gifts are not gifts unto themselves. All of our energy must be rooted in offering the kind of worship that heals wounded hearts.

To be gifted is not enough. To be a great singer or orator is not enough. We must be fresh! Galatians 5:22 lists the attributes of fruit. Love is the centerpiece of all spiritual things, but many of us focus more on the catchy phrases of a song than the love in our hearts. And that is why we are stale in his presence because our voice sounds good but our love expression is lacking. We are walking contradictions. We encourage people to embrace their families in church but we don't even talk to ours at home. We bless the Lord on Sunday, but curse others out on Monday. Yes, I know you can sing, but how is your spirit? Are you walking in love, joy, peace and longsuffering every day? Are you fresh in his presence, or is God reaching back in the bin for another, more suitable option?

Many of us have heard friends say "I love you," but their actions prove otherwise. Love must be fresh, and the same is true for the remaining fruits listed in Galatians. Just because someone has fruit doesn't mean God will choose them. Just because someone has a gift doesn't mean God wants it. God is looking for fresh worship. God wants concentrated time. What good would joy, peace, and longsuffering be if they all decayed before they were consumed? How much meekness and temperance do you really have if you're quick to lose your temper when things don't go your way? If they don't sing your song that day, or if the pastor decides to change up the flow of things in the service—how do you respond? With fruit, or in the flesh? How good is your fruit if it only tastes good when you have a microphone in your hand?

All of our energy must be rooted in offering the kind of worship that heals wounded hearts.

The point is, if you want to remain in Him, abide with him. Check the freshness of your fruit. Don't just pursue opportunities that look good to your eye. Make sure that you intend to remain in His Presence, or bow out gracefully. True worshippers are not satisfied with fruit alone. We live to offer fresh love, fresh joy, and fresh faith. The more time we spend with God, the fresher our fruit will be.

CHAPTER SIX
The Anointing verses Entitlement: The Mandate

The Spirit of the Lord is upon Me,
Because He has anointed Me
To preach the gospel to the poor;
He has sent Me to heal the brokenhearted,[a]
To proclaim liberty to the captives
And recovery of sight to the blind,
To set at liberty those who are oppressed;
(Luke 4:18)

Have you ever met a famous person who knew they were famous and wanted everyone else to know it too? We all know people like that— in their minds, they are the best thing since sliced bread, and they presume that you think the same way about them too. If you've ever met someone who is self-absorbed and narcissistic, how did your impression of them change later? What did you think of them after you saw them dressed in their true colors? The Bible says, "pride goes before destruction and a haughty spirit before a fall." One of the things many of us forget is that God hates pride. He hates those who live as if everything worships at their feet. He despises those who have assumed that the world must bow to them because of their gifts, talents, or fame. As a worship leader in the Lord's church, we must always remember that God is the one that we are called to make famous. We are not leaders because we are better than; we are leaders because we are responsible for. The moment you forget that is the moment you will confuse the anointing with entitlement.

A few years ago, the Lord spoke to my heart about our local assignment in the church. Every time I heard the word "assignment," I also heard the word "consecrate." Why? Because the level of your assignment must match the level of your consecration. The effectiveness of your sound is contingent upon the efficiency of your surrender. No surrender, no sound; just noise. No consecration, wasted assignment; just a gig. God wants to use you, but in order to maximize his glory within you, you've got to be set apart for his purpose. This is why there is a spiritual urging from God, in this season, for consecration and holiness. I know. I know. Holiness is a curse word in the church today, but remember, without holiness, no man can see God; which explains why so many people see you, but they don't see God. They hear our riffs, they like our runs, they know our chord progressions, and they repeat our beautiful songs, but they don't see God. They see our shape, our curves, and our designer outfits, but they don't see God. First things first: there must be consecration before there is a manifestation. God won't show up in a house that is too full of its own ego. God wants the center stage, and God is the only one to be adored.

HOW TO AVOID A POLLUTED SPIRIT

In order to maintain your anointing, consecration is a must. "Consecration" is a word that relates to cleansing our spiritual selves from the distractions of this world that try to pollute us and dilute us. When the enemy comes to pollute, he will use the lust of the eye or the lust of the flesh or the pride of life to add so much trash to our treasure, that we become unusable. And when the enemy tries to dilute us, he will try to mix his demonic scheme into the formula of God's purest stream within you. When spiritual water is diluted with the devil's ingredients, contamination is the result; and nobody wants to drink from a dirty well. This is why we must consistently give ourselves to a consecrated life before God.

Consecration is not a passive attempt. Consecration is a deliberate commitment to show GOD that we recognize how badly we need to make an effort to be close to His heart. Consecration is usually a time when we give ourselves a "spiritual laxative", as it were, to cleanse the walls of our heart from all of the junk, distractions and mess that has slowly but surely grasped a stronghold on our clarity. When we are not consecrated before God, we can't concentrate on the vision. And when the vision is distorted, the people have no direction.

WHO DO YOU THINK WE ARE?

We think we come to church for God to worship us. Or even worse, we assume that the glory of God won't come until we take the platform.

Back in the day, when a mother saw that her child was raising their voice at her, she would stop and look at the child with *that look* that only a mother could give. Then, she would follow up with the question: *who do you think you are?* When mama asked that question, you didn't need to answer. It was rhetorical. When mama asked that question, she was answering it at the same time. She was saying the answer without saying a word, but you knew what she wanted to say. In short, she wanted you to know that you were nothing without her. When she pointed to the incision near her stomach, that meant, "I brought you in this world, and I can take you out." Just who do you think you are? Mama asked that question when we were kids, but God is asking that question to us now.

How does pollution enter into our spirit? Pollution happens when we forget who we are. We think we come to church for God to worship us. Or even worse, we assume that the glory of God won't come until we take the platform. This is the problem. Pollution enters through the door of entitlement. Over the last few years, I have been watching and listening to a people who are displaying a spirit that is so strong and extremely flesh-driven. A strong spirit of "entitlement" is pervading our ministries. Entitlement is seen in our attitudes with one another, in our marriages, and in our relationships, etc. Every time I try to overlook it, the Holy Ghost keeps showing it to me. Entitlement rears its head when you will fight to preach in the pulpit but you never want to serve in the neighborhood. Entitlement shows up when you expect people to reach out to you but you don't out-reach to anyone else.

...you may receive applause from man but have you received an ovation from the Lord?

Something is wrong with this picture; especially because as the church (derived from the Greek word *ecclesia*) we are supposed to be the called out ones; sent by God to go to the uttermost parts of the earth to spread the gospel by any means necessary. If you're too entitled to go to certain places in order to preach the gospel, then you should not be permitted to go anywhere. Jesus sat among them all: sinners, lepers, women with blood issues, Pharisees, Sadducees, court officials, fisherman, prostitutes, blind men, dumb men, demons, angels—it didn't matter. He didn't limit his ministry to only feeding the five thousand for recognition. He was often seen in small groups telling other people not to reveal his true identity to the world. Jesus was humble; and if we are called to represent him, we must be and do the same. Sadly, entitlement has become our kryptonite. We have become so addicted to the gigantic platform that we have forgotten where our calling comes from—our call belongs to and comes from the Lord. Power belongs to and comes from the Lord. Promotion belongs to and comes from the Lord. If God is not lifted up, no one will be drawn toward Him or the church. If you are lifted up, you may receive applause from man but have you received an ovation from the Lord?

NEVER FORGET YOUR PLACE

Worship leaders, never forget that the platform on which you stand is only stable because of the price Jesus paid on the cross. It was because of his death, burial, and resurrection that we have the power and the permission to speak on his behalf. Visibility is great. But you weren't elevated in worship leadership to be visible; you were elevated to be responsible. What God has afforded us (whatever it may be) is a result of His grace and trust. When people recognize you in the mall or at the gas station, don't let the helium in your balloon cause your ego to swell. It is in Him that we live, move and have our being. When the inflation of flesh swells in the presence of God, there can be no manifestation of miracles, signs and wonders. There can be no weight of glory. There can be no true worship. At best, we are mimicking or imitating real presence. At worst, we are moved by emotions and therefore, deceiving ourselves.

CONSECRATION YIELDS COMPASSION

The Bible Says in Matthew 9:36, "When Jesus saw the multitude that was scattered like sheep with no Shepherd, He moved with compassion and he helped them..." It is a major problem when our passion for the things that hurt God's heart are not the things that hurt our hearts. It is a major problem when we allow someone to lead us to a place that they've never been themselves. These kinds of things happen (a loss of compassion and a loss of direction) when we cease from consistent fellowship with our Creator. If you are not praying, then you are an atheist dressed in church paraphernalia. You look like a Christian, and you may even sound like a Christian, but true Christians communicate with their Creator. True Christians talk to their Lord and Savior. If you do not believe in God, then you will not talk to God; and if you are not talking to God, then it is impossible to have a relationship with God. So, yes, you may be able to sing; and yes, you may be an amazing musician, but if you do not pray to the God about whom you sing, you are an atheist in Christian paraphernalia.

In prayer, God clarifies the call and reveals the assignment. The secret place of prayer is the place where wisdom and strength are perfected in our hearts.

Prayer is the access code that God has given us to touch Him and to hear from Him. It is the place of direction and instruction for our lives. It's the avenue where God tells us who is permitted to be in our space, and who must depart from our space. In prayer, God clarifies the call and reveals the assignment. The secret place of prayer is the place where wisdom and strength are perfected in our hearts. When you pray, you see the need for consecration because God shows you who you really are. Prayer is like looking into the mirror—the longer you look, the more you will find areas of discoloration, disconnection, and disintegration.

THE HOLY GHOST IS YOUR HELPER

One of my favorite scriptures speaks to the place that we as leaders are called to maintain. It's Psalm 63, which says," Oh God, You are my God. Early will I seek you, I long for You; I thirst for you in a dry land where there is no water". *A dry land where there is no water.* Whenever you see water, wind or oil in the scriptures, it signifies that the presence of the Holy Ghost is there to make an impact. And the psalmist is saying I seek you and long for you because when I don't, I am dry. When I don't, there is no presence or Spirit or power. Let me just drop this nugget here for us to consider. The person of the Holy Ghost is, in its translation, the Advocate, The Mediator, The Paraclete and the Reminder. The Holy Ghost is the help that acts as your spirit-interpreter given by GOD. It is virtually impossible to serve GOD without the intercession of the Holy Ghost. And what God has shown me is that many of us are operating in skill, gifting and "know how," but we are void of the access to the empowering presence of the Holy Ghost. That is why there is so much struggle and frustration in areas that shouldn't have struggle or frustration. That is why there is so much division in our churches—it's very subtle, but trust me, it's there.

How do you vacuum out the division? You call a consecration. Directors of Worship and Pastors of Worship, designate a specific time for prayer and fasting. Be deliberate about having an intense season of intercession. Make sure that all parties involved in the worship experience are included (musicians, singers, dancers, drama, etc.) When you clean your spirit, God will bless your house. When you dedicate concentrated time to consecrate yourself before God, you will see results almost immediately. Entitlement will exit, and the anointing will enter. If you study the anointing in Scripture, you will see that the word anointing is always in direct correlation with worship. You can't really worship God through Christ, the Anointed One, if there is no God-presence. So, I have learned that pure worship is a result of the anointing of God being released on a vessel who has yielded everything in order to get into the presence. In other words, there is an expectation of a supernatural visitation and manifestation wherever praise and worship are given under a verifiable anointing.

I have also learned that, in order to operate under the anointing, there must first be sensitivity to the spirit of the Lord and the power of the spirit. The Bible says that the spirit of the Holy Ghost is always making intercession for us. The reality is we are flesh, and for that reason, we can't understand the things of the spirit. But, in order for the anointing to flow and move, there must always be a consecrated vessel set aside to hear directly from the heart of God through the Holy Ghost. Isaiah 10:27 declares that the anointing does two major things as it relates to spiritual warfare; it lifts burdens and it destroys yokes. This is important because it speaks again to the need for consecration. When you consecrate yourself, you remove entitlement and replace it with the anointing. And in this last hour, we must understand that spiritual warfare is as real today as it was in days of old. According to Ephesians 2:2, Satan is still the prince of the air. And this is where spiritual warfare takes place.

Real war happens up above your head, but thanks be to God, we serve the King of Kings. So even the prince of the air has to bow down to the King!

GOD WANTS TO DO A NEW THING

Why am I saying this, Because God wants to do a new thing in his church. If we are to live a life of worship so that there are signs and wonders that follow our lives, then there must be an anointing placed on us in our worship. The anointing is the empowerment of the Holy Spirit. It is something that happens within you. The anointing will affect everything you do and everything you say because it is the smearing of God's presence and His power in, by and through the Holy Ghost. According to the prophet Isaiah, in pure worship (stemming from an anointed presence) there are a number of things that will happen: (Isaiah 61 & Luke 4)

1.   *Brokenhearted people will be healed*

2.   *Captives or enslaved people will be delivered*

3.   *Blind people will receive sight*

4.   *Oppressed, or down-trodden people will be set free*

There will always be fruit from your labor when the anointing of the Anointed one, Christ, has been invoked in and through the worship. In order to live in this anointing, there must be a daily visitation in fellowship and intimacy with God through Christ, The Anointed one and His anointing, and the Holy Ghost must be comfortable to dine, dwell, and linger with you. Then and only then can Christ release a presence that remains with you long after the song has been sung, and long after the service has ended. The Bible says in I Cor 5:17, " Therefore, If any man be in Christ, the Anointed one, he is a new creation; old things have passed away; behold all things have become new." Old things include our old ways of thinking and our old attitudes. Everything about us changes when we get into pure worship and a fresh anointing which only comes with relationship with Christ. You'll find yourself singing, "I can see clearly now the rain is gone."

Finally, we must understand that God is so specific about our lives that He will not give you your neighbors anointing. However, we all can have the same anointing that Jesus had when he began to preach the message about the anointing in Luke 4:18 &19. An anointing to heal broken hearts, an anointing to preach deliverance, an anointing that will give sight to the blind and an anointing that will preach liberty to those who are oppressed. There is an anointing on us being poured into our vessel and God wants to lift us to heights unknown. I'm telling you: the only thing that is going to defeat this war against the enemy is the anointing. Drugs, sickness, disease and abuse of all kinds are around us. On every level we are being affected by the war of sin. The bible says, the enemy whose plan is to steal, to kill and destroy our existence is attacking us on every side. However, there is victory because of Christ and His anointing is greater in us than he that is in the world. Some trust in horses and some trust in chariots, but I trust in the name of the Lord. Saints, the name of the Lord is still a strong tower. This is the place where we will find our refuge and security.

Fill my cup Lord. I lift it up Lord.
Come and fill this thirsting In my soul.
Bread of heaven feed me 'til I want no more.
Fill my cup, fill it up and make me whole.

In the words of one songwriter, " We need an outpour of the spirit of the Holy God of Israel. Send it down. Send it down. We need it, we need it Lord." And yes, like never before, we need the smearing of the presence of the Lord Jesus Christ in our lives. There is no way to go higher in God except we allow our minds and our spirits to change. As the scripture says in Romans 12, we need to be transformed and not conformed to the world. Conformed = to be made to do. Transformed = to be persuaded to blend or fit in with or to be shaped into something or someone by the Holy Ghost.

Finally it is important to consider this school of thought. The anointing is radiant and causes one to glow with the presence of God. You who are anointed must guard your anointing. The anointing will allow prophecy to flow. The anointing is heightened in praise. The anointing attracts, pulls and has certain energy. People are attracted to light. Remember, my friends, the anointing highlights. The oil will flow when you let go in God's presence. When the Holy Ghost influences your life, it will reflect in your life, and all will know that God lives here.

Consecrate me now to Thy service Lord
by your power of grace divine
Let my soul look up with a steadfast hope
and my will be Lost in Thine
Draw me nearer near oh blessed Lord
to the cross where Thou hast died
Draw me nearer near oh blessed Lord
to thy precious bleeding side

CHAPTER SEVEN

Intercession:
The Highest Form of Worship
Leadership

*If my people, who are called by my name, will humble
themselves and pray and seek my face and turn from
their wicked ways, then I will hear from heaven, and
I will forgive their sin and will heal their land. Now my
eyes will be open and my ears attentive to the prayers
offered in this place. I have chosen and consecrated
this temple so that my Name may be there forever. My
eyes and my heart will always be there.*
(2 Chronicles 7:14-15)

If you've ever had to go to the airport or the train station,
especially when you're in a foreign country, you could
rely on a customer service area where people are
paid to provide one service: to give you direction. These
people have been trained to get you to your destination.
These people are typically fluent in many languages,
and they are also more educated about the location
than you are. It is their job to direct you, guide you, and
assist you so that you don't miss your flight. Many of these
customer service representatives are very nice, but it's
a horrible thing when the person who is supposed to
help you is mean, frustrated, and ready to go home. It's
frustrating when you go to them for help, and they cut
you off in the middle of your sentence without getting

clarity. People who are in a rush don't need this job. People who don't like people shouldn't apply for this job. Why, because your safe arrival is contingent upon their direction.

You probably think you know where I am going with this, but I am about to shock you. Prayer is the key to accessing the presence of God. No prayer, no power. No prayer, no direction. So, like the customer service center at an airport or train station, every day, as God's worship leader, we must check in to the center, and ask him for direction. If we don't, others may be lost. If we don't, others will not know how to access the glory because we are working for the Lord, but asleep on the job. We are supposed to be the place where they can come and receive translation, communication, direction, and guidance. But if we are attitudinal, they won't get the help they need. If we are just singing for the check, the people won't get to their destination. If we are operating under entitlement and not under the anointing, we have left innocent lives without a compass by which to find God.

Prayer is the fuel station that restores and refills your overloaded soul. Prayer is the resource center that reveals the mysteries of godliness.

AFTER THE SONG IS OVER, DO YOU PRAY?

Always know that we must be willing to serve as the place where people can come and ask us for directions. This means, above our gifts and talents, we are called to be prayer warriors and intercessors. As a prayer warrior, you must cultivate a daily routine of worship and prayer with God. When you refuse to pray, you are operating on empty. Prayer is the fuel station that restores and refills your overloaded soul. Prayer is the resource center that reveals the mysteries of godliness. The song of the Lord is revealed in prayer. The sound of God is discovered in prayer. When you run to rehearsal to sing without entering into his presence through prayer, you treat church as if it is a gig, and there is no demand of glory in the room because prayer sets the tone. Make no mistake about it: praying is the most essential component to a consecrated soul. When you pray, God hears and is faithful to respond.

Consider one of the most popular verses on prayer. 2 Chronicles 7:14 says, "if my people, who are called by my name, will humble themselves and pray, and seek my face, and turn from their wicked ways, then I will hear from heaven, and forgive their sins, and heal their land." This scripture is packed with pre-requisites that God requires of us before we mount the sacred stage in his name. First, we've got to be humble. People who are full of pride will never get a prayer through. Why, Because God hates pride. And at best, your prayer will be heard by others but will be muted by God.

A humble spirit is a lowly spirit. A humble spirit is a teachable spirit. God won't hear a know-it-all spirit, because if you think you know it all, you will enter into the prayer room with the wrong posture. You will talk to God as if he is your administrative assistant, and God doesn't work for you.

ARE YOU HUMBLE?

So, Chronicles says for us to first examine our posture. The next time you have a small group bible study with trusted friends, ask them this question: am I humble? Ask them to give you their honest opinion about your humility and posture. If they hesitate when answering the question that means you've got something to work on. Now remember, I said ask your trusted friends—not people who don't know the real you; not people who want your position, but ask people who have your best interest at heart. Ask them if you are humble. Most of us know whether we are humble or not but it's always good to get another perspective.

God says after you humble yourself, then you can pray. The pre-requisite to prayer is humility. And the pre-requisite to seeking God's face is to pray with your heart. Here is an example of a prayer that I would like to recommend for you. It is a daily declaration and it is something that will guide your prayers so that you are reminded of the power of God in and through your life— not just for your personal needs, but for the world.

Today I prayed that GOD would help me to hear His
voice, respond and
live in the sound of victory
Today I prayed that GOD's strength would help my
weaknesses and show
me Courage to resist the pull of the enemy
Today I prayed that the enemies of hell wouldn't
prosper over me and
that God would cover me, even if the enemy is me
Today I prayed that my concerns and cares were the
same as His
Today I prayed that fear would be conquered and
Faith would soar like
an eagle above high mountains

Today I prayed for my friends; that their dreams and
aspirations would
come to pass as it pleased GOD
Today I prayed for my family that they might come to
know the love of

JESUS in power and in truth
Today I prayed for Sickness and Disease all over the world and I
called on the healing power of GOD through my Lord Jesus Christ to
arrest it and bring HEALING
Today I prayed for children of all races, denominations and nations
around the world that GOD would keep them pure and unharmed
Today I prayed for Presidents, Governors, leaders and Spiritual
leaders all over the world that God's wisdom would be their portion

Today I prayed for the PEACE OF JERUSALEM
Today I prayed for Africa the mother continent and all the people
there in the country
Today I prayed for racism, sexism and classism and that God would
fill us with his love that will make us ONE
Today I prayed for the poor and GOD told me that they'll be with us
always...

Today I prayed for habits and addictions that GOD would release
Wholeness to the men and women who struggle that they might depend on
HIM as their source and resource
Today I prayed for husbands and wives that the bond and union He put
together would be restored with Grace and LOVE
Today I prayed for the single sister and the single

brother that they
would enjoy the season of SOLO LIFE, count it as a
blessing and not a
curse
Today I prayed that we could posture ourselves that
WHATEVER our lot we
would declare in faith that IT IS WELL in Christ Jesus Our
Lord!!!

Today I prayed that my worship would outweigh worry
Today I prayed that peace would sustain us and cause
despair to
surrender,
Today I prayed that as Jesus Prayed for Peter that his
faith would not
fail, that He, Christ Jesus, would pray for me

Today I prayed............

If you can commit to declaring this prayer once a day, you have already set the tone for God to intervene in your daily activities. If you can discipline yourself to pray in the morning before you rush out of the house, and at night before you go to sleep, you have guarded your dreams, thoughts, and daily commitments in prayer, and as you go about your day, you will see how impactful a consistent prayer life is. This is what 2 Chronicles tells us God will do when we humble ourselves, pray, and seek his face. But that's not all we must do. Before God can intervene on our behalf, we have to be willing to turn from our wicked ways. We have a lot of worship leaders who pray in public, but are still doing their dirt in private. And to this, God says: he won't hear you. God won't hear the prayers of those who want to present an image of holiness, or a form of godliness in front of others, but in the background, they are living a hot mess. Now, don't get me wrong: all of us have sinned and fallen short. If it weren't for the grace of God, none of us would be able to lead the people into a place of worship. But there is a difference between someone who is struggling with their thorn, and someone who is taking advantage of God's grace. When you refuse to try, and when you make up your mind that you are going to do what you want without any level of honor to God's expectations, God is not obligated to hear your prayer. He is not obligated to display his glory.

God wants your heart, not just your gift, He wants to lead your life, not just save it.

Why; Because, God knows the secrets of the heart. And He knows your motives and your intentions, and if you are unwilling to turn, then He is unwilling to respond.

After we turn from our wicked ways, then God will hear, forgive and heal. What if healing isn't happening in our churches because we aren't turning from our wicked ways? What if we aren't turning from our wicked ways because we aren't praying to the God who can reveal those wicked ways? You see my friend everything affects something else. When you humble yourself, you realize how much you need God to succeed. That realization alone will cause you to pray and seek God's face in everything. When you live a surrendered life to God, it is an every-day experience. Everyday you are looking to please God. Everyday you are searching for God's voice. Everyday, you wake up and attempt to live better for the sake of the gospel. All of this will inspire you to turn from your wicked ways so that God can hear, forgive and heal. Some of us have prayed but we haven't turned. And until we turn, our words are empty tradition. Our songs are filled with rhetorical hypocrisy. God wants your heart, not just your gift. He wants to lead your life, not just save it. By praying to God, you are reporting to the supervisor of all existence, so that when the people come to the house of God, you can direct them to the well that never runs dry.

INTERCESSION: THE HIGHEST FORM OF WORSHIP

This is one component of worship. But the highest form of worship is intercession. Intercession is the ability to pray on the behalf of someone else. Intercession is a self-less discipline. It requires you to be so selfless that you forget about your problems, and go to God on behalf of anothers' problems. When you look up the word "intercession" in a Bible Dictionary, you will see that this term was first introduced to us via the prophets of the Old Testament. Prophets were "repairers of the breach" and their primary responsibility was to stand between the holes in the wall to protect the city, country, or region from further demolition. Literally, these soldiers would stand between the area that needed repair because their presence was like cement on the wall. They had to stand in the place of the wall because if they didn't, the enemy could find the loophole and terrorize the land. How does that relate to us? I'm glad you asked. As ministry leaders in the Lord's church, we must see our role as more than activity-driven. We are purposed to function as a wall to keep the holes covered. We are intercessors before we are singers. We are intercessors before we are preachers, dancers, actors, performers, artists, ministers, or ushers. Before we take our post, we must intercede on behalf of the flock to which God has called us to serve.

> Our responsibility as leaders is not just to get attention. Our call is to stand in the gap for those who don't even know that their walls are damaged.

We must be selfless and intentional about locating the spiritual abscess in the house and filling it with our prayer. It is a contradiction for us to worship a God who we haven't seen in the flesh, but to ignore our brother and sister who we see every day. We know they are going through, but we won't stop to pray for their marriage. We know they are struggling financially, but we won't pause to intervene on their behalf. Intercession is more important than you know. Every time we intercede, we are reminded of what Christ did for us. Christ knew no sin but became sin for us. He literally took on our sin, endured our penalty, and before he died on the cross, he asked the Father to forgive them; to forgive us. If this isn't intercession, I don't know what is. Our responsibility as leaders is not just to get attention. Our call is to stand in the gap for those who don't even know that their walls are damaged. We must lift up our pastors and leadership team. They are often overwhelmed with the need to show up for the congregation, but who will show up for them? Who is praying for the pastor's wife who has to share her husband with the church every week? Who is praying for the children of the pastor, who didn't ask to be born into a family like this, but they still need to know who they are without trying to turn their calling into their parents'? Who is praying for the musicians who will play for hours to make sure you get your praise on, but they may be struggling with knowing Jesus for themselves? As worship leaders, we are spiritual customer service representatives. When people walk into the church, it's no different than tourists or visitors walking into the airport. Some people know which terminal they need to go to, but most of us have no clue what we need. We know that we are in transition but we need to trust those who have been appointed over us as leaders to guide us, motivate us, teach us, and intercede for us. The best thing about intercession is that it's not about you. The best thing about worship is that it's not about you. That is why intercession is the highest form of worship; because when you do it, God is at the center of it all.

CHAPTER EIGHT

The Posture, the Platform, and the Privilege of Worship

In a recent interview, President Barack Obama was asked to describe what it was like to be the President of the United States. They asked him, "How does it feel to be the most powerful man in the free world? How does it feel to have a limousine take you everywhere, and a private plane that can fly you anywhere in the world that you want to go?" To this, Obama responded, "it feels like... responsibility; a lot of responsibility. I do not gloat in my position because I do not work for myself; I work for the American people. I am the President, but the people are my boss." Obama understood something that many of us are still struggling to comprehend: leadership is work. Leadership means you will have to sacrifice something in order to lead well. To be God's chosen vessel, you will be expected to live with a different set of standards. You will never have the luxury of privacy.

> ...it is God who hired you, but it is the church that trusts you.

Much like the President, everything you do is seen by God. The Bible declares that the eyes of the Lord are in every place. Let us not forget that it is God who hired you, but it is the church that trusts you. You are not the mediator between the people and God, but you are certainly a symbol of Christ before the people.

You are called to be an example. You are called to stand out. You are not just standing before the people because you are gifted. Your character must also reflect the heart of Jesus. Your speech must sound like the life Jesus led, and your leadership must pull people close to Jesus. Jesus knew what he was called to do, but it took him 30 years to prepare for it. Do you get that? It took Jesus thirty years of preparation for three years of demonstration. So why are so many of our praise leaders frustrated because they can't sing their song the day after they have joined the team? Why are we so impatient? I'll tell you why, Because nobody taught us about the process of preparation. Nobody taught us how to wait on the Lord. Nobody taught us that the Lord will make room for your gift when your character is ready for the platform. Every leader worth his or her salt must be prepared. Every leader must be made ready for the process that is required to serve on behalf of God for the people. You are not in power so that you can gloat. You are not in leadership so you can boast or name-drop. You are in position so that you can promote Christ. It's not our agenda; it's his agenda.

If only we could have that same perspective as it relates to leading God's people. If only we could practice loving the way Jesus loved the church. He loved us so much that he died for us. His leadership was not about the platform. It wasn't about the notoriety. It was about service. Jesus said, "Let the greatest one among you be a servant." I fear for our 21st Century Church because many of us want to be a celebrity, but most of us don't want to be a servant. But if we would just take on the heart of Jesus, and live in a way that mirrors Jesus, we will always please God.

HOW YOU DEFINE WORSHIP, SAYS A LOT

As an icebreaker exercise, I want you to ask your pastor what his definition of worship is. I want you to ask him what his vision for worship is, and then, I want you to ask the team to define worship in their own words. I've discovered over the years that how you define something says a lot about the way you see something. Many people define LOVE as an action word, but they have to prove it through their deeds in order for LOVE to be LOVE. In the same way, worship is a popular term in church but don't be surprised by this fact: many people define worship differently.

A few months ago, I was having a conversation with my friend Vashawn Mitchell, and he began to emphasize on "the more" that worship brings into your life. He began asking our praise team, "do you want more of this or that" and he opened up John 4 in a way that I will never forget. In order for you to really understand the posture, the platform, and the privilege of worship, you must want MORE spirit and more truth. When you study the word *Spirit* more closely, you will discover that in Hebrew, spirit is translated *"ruah"* which in its primary sense means *breath, air,* and *wind.* When he formed mankind, he used his breath. In the upper room, the breath and wind of God revealed itself in such a strong way that the people of God had an unforgettable encounter. All throughout the Bible, we see pictures of wind in connection to worship. Jesus indeed uses the sensory image of the wind to suggest to Nicodemus that he needs to experience the newness of life. This life can only come when God personally breathes into us, and we are born again by divine spirit. In English copies of the Bible, the word "spirit" occurs 823 times. It's first occurrence is Genesis 1:2. The "Spirit" occurs most often in the Old Testament book of Isaiah and the New Testament book of Acts. The Hebrew word translated is *ruach*. The Greek word is *pneuma*. In addition, the phrase "spirit of God" is reasonably rendered "Breath of God" or "Wind of God." The word "spirit" has taken on a corporeal tone like the word "ghost." Likely, if the word PNEUMA had been rendered "breath" or "wind" in English, the Holy Spirit would not have developed so strongly in English as a Person part of the Trinitarian Godhead. Some translators actually do render RUACH as "wind" in Genesis 1:2, where GOD demonstrates to us what happens when he breathes or His wind is engaged in us. In short, WE BECOME A LIVING SOUL.

Why is this important for the posture we must take on as worship leaders? Because if you think that your breath is yours, then you will then that God's people are yours. At best, your breath is borrowed from heaven. Your life is a lease from above, and God can take his breath back whenever he wants to. It is grace, then, that allows us to drive a vehicle that doesn't belong to us. It is grace that allows us to lead people with the breath that God has dispensed into us. When we understand the posture of God's spirit, then we won't try to dictate how he can move in the midst of his people. But let's go even deeper.

Did you know that the word WORSHIP is first demonstrated in Genesis 4:2-5? Let's look at two things here DEMONSTRATION & PREPARATION. Cain and Abel were brothers and whether we know it or not, this was the first lesson ever given on worship. Some people have suggested that Cain's offering was unacceptable because he offered plants while Abel offered animals. But I don't think this was the case, since God accepted grain offerings at other times (Lev. 2) and since the laws regarding sacrifices had not yet been given (though it is interesting to note that Abel offered fat portions as prescribed in the Levitical law - see Lev. 3). It's possible that Cain and Abel had received some instruction on what constituted an acceptable sacrifice from God, or that Cain had committed other wrongs that would make his offering unacceptable to God. However, the passage does give us some clues about what God wants. It says that Abel "brought fat portions from some of the firstborn." He offered some of what came first, as opposed to waiting until an animal had plenty of offspring (and the oldest were reproducing themselves). So instead of sacrificing one of the youngest,

At best, your breath is borrowed from heaven. Your life is a lease from above, and God can take his breath back whenever he wants to.

he offered the choicest parts. Abel was clearly giving the best of what he had to God. Cain, on the other hand, brought "some of the fruits of the soil," which were not necessarily the best crops - they may have been damaged and/or been what Cain considered "extra" or "leftover." Abel's and Cain's actions were a reflection of their attitudes towards God - should God receive the best of what they had or not? - And it was their attitudes that God was concerned with.

This all connects to the posture of your heart. You can't maintain the platform of worship if your posture is off. Even if you offer something to God, it doesn't mean God has to accept it. I hear you ask why? It's simply because the key word here is offering. If you study Old Testament Scriptures, especially the book of Leviticus, The word OFFERING means to *draw near*. The word offering is synonymous with the word demonstration. David said it best in 2 Samuel 24:24, "... I will not offer to God that which has cost me nothing". In other words, your worship must be an offering that comes from you to GOD. It must cost you something. It must cost you labor. It must cost you convenience. It must draw from you that which can be seen as the best of you because God doesn't want our sloppy seconds.

And while I'm here, let me park for a second to say this: worship is not a song that is slow, fast, in a major key or in a minor key. More accurately, worship is presenting an offering to God that he desires to breathe on. Thus, if you present an offering to GOD that is leftovers, or an offering that is without sacrifice for you, then God is not obligated to respond to you. Why? Remember, *it is not worship if a sacrifice isn't involved.* I've said it before and I will say it again: worship only becomes worship when GOD responds! So, if you sing great songs and God doesn't respond, you sounded great but it is not worship. If you pray and shoot out a bunch of great words and phrases and God doesn't respond, it's not worship. Or if you preach or read scripture or dance and GOD doesn't respond, then it's not worship.

Worship comes with a responsibility. The platform comes with a responsibility. The privilege of worship acknowledges the responsibility. Or might I say the call as a Leader of worship has a responsibility. Let's look at a passage in Ezekiel 44. I see a few phrases that grab me immediately. When God says things more than once, it is to be taken very seriously. And he says a few times here, "Mark Well Son of Man". In other words PAY ATTENTION, THIS IS IMPORTANT, THIS IS SERIOUS BUSINESS HERE. What is God trying to say? In short, he's saying "don't play with worship." Real worship in the presence of the Almighty God will cause you to do self-examination. Real worship will cause you to repent and turn from your wicked ways. Real worship will make you ask for forgiveness from people who don't even deserve an apology. If you study the Scriptures, you will discover that the priests and the Levites were deliberate about following God's every request as it related to worship. They didn't want to distract or take away from the glory that was to belong to God. We discuss this all the time, and even though these are very elementary teachings, they are important to discuss when you think about the platform you stand on every Sunday:

Ladies: too small and shows us all
            The attack of the Rack

Men: Let me show you my little friend
            Hefty Hefty His Sack

THE POSITION OF A WORSHIP LEADER

As we look to discover the Biblical purpose of the Worship leader, there are a few questions that we need to ask in order to get a better understanding of the purpose and the function of this position. This is not a position that is based on the popularity or the Charisma of an individual. This position is an appointment that should be made by the Senior Pastor of the Local church body. It is a position that should be considered in Prayer and fasting. There are certain attributes of the Worship Leader that are very important to the growth and development of the Corporate Worship setting called the local church.

If we look at the Old Testament scripture we see that King David made appointments that were not based on popularity or family connection. However, the persons he appointed were "Skillful", which is to say that the person who is to lead music, must be apt to learn. There are a few considerations for this position one must consider in the scripture.

1.   *Leviticus 8 & 9* Moses consecrates Aaron and his sons for the appointment.

2.   *Numbers 8:5-26* the period of listening and learning from God. This requires much quiet time and fasting. This is a period of sanctification.

3.   *I Chronicles 6:31&32* It is an appointment that must be served according to order.

4.   *I Chronicles 23:2-32* To assist the Ecclesia of the church and to help articulate the heart of the Senior Pastor and the Leadership of the house.

The person or persons chosen to lead worship must be apt to teach and articulate the vision and the heart of their pastor. He or she must spend time with the Pastor consistently to hear their heart and to create the picture to the congregation. This is not to take the place of the relationship between the Pastor and the Minister of Music.

There must be a perpetual anticipation of the inhabitation of the power of God in our worship services. However, if the atmosphere is not charged in praise, then we block the entrance of the glory of God.

The Praise and Worship leader must depend very heavily on the leading of the Holy Ghost. It is vital to the growth of the church that the faith of the leader is consistent with and parallel to the written word of God. Faith is the access key to the operation of signs and wonders following them that believe. There must be a perpetual anticipation of the inhabitation of the power of God in our worship services. However, if the atmosphere is not charged in praise, then we block the entrance of the glory of God. Atmosphere changing is the responsibility of the Praise and Worship leader in the spiritual realm. According to II Corinthians 10:3-5 Paul the writer teaches us to be aware that the atmosphere we fight in is not carnal, but spiritual. The weapons we use to conquer the enemy must be spiritual not carnal. So, understanding the spiritual realm is very important in the life of a called and appointed worship leader.

Finally, as the relationship with God and the Worship leader matures, the sound of the voice of God matures in the ear of the servant. That is what the worship leader is to the life of the people of God: a servant. This is how the chapter began, and this is how we must end. When you start, you must serve. When you end, you must serve. If you're singing one Sunday or sitting the next Sunday, you must serve. There must be covenant devotion made in the heart and in the life of the Worship Leader. This appointment cannot be based on skill and ability alone. It must be considered according to one's maturity in the things of God. And, we must always remember that, like a doctor, the lives of the people are in the hands of the Praise and Worship Leader.

So I ask you again: are you really sure you are prepared for the posture, the platform, and the position of worship? I encourage all persons handling the things of God, especially His people, to consider Nadab and Abihu, Aaron's sons, in Lev 10. We cannot come into the presence of God without going through preparation, consecration and sanctification. Only then will we be ready vessels prepared for the express service that will build the kingdom of God here on earth, as it is in heaven.

As you continue to read lift this song up to Jesus: "I surrender all I surrender all. All to Thee my blessed Savior. I surrender all"

CHAPTER NINE
A Consecrated Soul

Therefore, I urge you, brothers and sisters, in view of God's mercy, to offer your bodies as a living sacrifice, holy and pleasing to God—this is your true and proper worship. Do not conform to the pattern of this world, but be transformed by the renewing of your mind. Then you will be able to test and approve what God's will is—his good, pleasing and perfect will. (Romans 12:1-2)

I love holidays. I love birthdays. I love celebrations. I love festivals! It's just something about the love shared between family and friends over a homemade meal that warms my heart. I'm sure you love holidays, too; especially if someone in your family really knows how to cook. Take, for instance, Thanksgiving. My friends know that I will NOT go to just anybody's house for thanksgiving. I need to make sure that you know how to throw down! Or else, I will gladly escort myself to someone else's house. Those meals served during thanksgiving are not microwaveable meals. To really enjoy the food, it has to be prepared over time. Most people begin a week in advance for a meal that will take minutes to eat, but still, they take days to prepare it. Why? Because real food takes time to cook. Healthy food takes time to marinate. The longer you season, prep, and bake, the better the result will be in the end.

SOME THINGS TAKE TIME

I wish more worship leaders would use the slow cooker more than they did the microwave these days. Everybody wants success fast. They want fame immediately. They don't want to wait for the season to ripen them for the moment they are called to. We like shortcuts nowadays. If there's a direct flight, we want it. Even if it costs double the price that a layover costs, we will pay more to get where we want to get faster! And this is my concern for the direction we are headed in as a church. Back in the day, the saints were consecrated—not just in their bodies, but in their souls. Back in the day, when people had to preach, they would fast for two or three days and wait on the Lord for a word. Nowadays, we just get up and rattle off to the people whatever we heard on the Word Network, or we recycle a sermon we preached somewhere else. Back in the day, when the choir was going to sing for a revival, the director would call a fast. We would have shut-ins where the people would come and pray all night until the glory of the Lord showed up. The mothers and fathers of the church knew something that we are still struggling to comprehend: some things take time. You can't rush into the presence of God and rush out expecting a divine moment to happen. You've got to exercise patience and wait on the Lord! The Upper Room experience would've never happened if the gathered people didn't have the patience to wait. But if we have to wait ten minutes for service to begin, we are grabbing our phones, sending emails, checking social media, and doing everything except the thing we came into the house

> ...some things take time. You can't rush into the presence of God and rush out expecting a divine moment to happen.

of God for: worship.

Let me ask you some hard questions. When is the last time you took a few days to get away with Jesus? When is the last time you fasted without the pastor calling a fast? How often do you shut down the phone, the television and all other distractions just to align yourself with God? When is your daily devotional time? How faithful are you to keeping that time sanctified for God, and God alone? When was the last time you were so overwhelmed by God's presence that you lingered there for more than three hours?

CONSECRATION RECHARGE

If you're struggling to answer some of these questions, I think you're in desperate need of a consecration recharge. A few months ago, I sensed the need to consecrate and I wrote these words to my worship department. If these words inspire you, I want you to use this as a template and begin your own consecration journey. This is what I said:

Today is the beginning of the washing of our souls and our spirits. This fast will cause our flesh to be silent as our spirit takes a leap to come closer to GOD our father. Remember the pattern for answered prayer when you pray according to Matthew 6:10: WORSHIP, WILL, and then, articulate your WANTS. I request that you pray for the following:

1. Pray for clarity in the will of GOD for your life, your family, your peace of mind

2. Pray for those who are your co-workers and co laborers in the ministry

3. Pray for your Pastor and the assignment he/she has locally/nationally.

4. Pray for the President and the leaders of our county, state and country.

5. Thank GOD FOR A JOB THAT IS A RESOURCE FOR NEEDS, Hallelujah, and Thank Him for being our SOURCE for ALL THINGS.

As you study the word, develop a habit of studying the Gospels (Matthew, Mark, Luke & John) so you can open up your understanding to the life of our Savior. Take time to let the Word of the Lord wash over you each day. Purchase a journal and commit to 7 days, 21 days, or 40 days of consecration. Each day, write down the scripture you read and how God spoke to you. Begin each day reciting this Psalm until you have memorized it:

Psalm 145: 1-5

1 I will extol You, my God, O King;
	And I will bless Your name forever and ever.
2 Every day I will bless You,
	And I will praise Your name forever and ever.
3 Great is the LORD, and greatly to be praised;
	And His greatness is unsearchable.
4 One generation shall praise Your works to another,
	And shall declare Your mighty acts.
5 I will meditate on the glorious splendor of Your majesty,

And on Your wondrous works
Next, I want you to enter into a voluntary season of Fasting and Prayer. When you do, it will be a time of soul cleansing and a time of Spirit strengthening. It is important that you also understand that according to the scriptures, fasting is a private offering that we present to GOD for an outward manifestation. Do not announce to the world that you are fasting. Keep some things a secret and bask in God's presence, asking anything in His name with the confidence that He will do it!

Here are some scriptures that will help you to get a clearer understanding of where God wants to take you. As you prepare for this season of consecration, celebrate the victories that GOD will release into your life as you present yourself as an offering to Him.

Psalm 24:3-5

3) WHO may ascend into the hill of the Lord? Or who may stand in His holy place?
4) He who has clean hands and a pure heart Who has not lifted his soul to an idol. Nor sworn deceitfully.
5) He shall receive the blessing from the Lord, And Righteousness from the GOD of his salvation

My prayer is that we move to a place that God's spirit and His power is fresh in us and on us from day to day. I pray that God will give answers to prayers in your life and in your family. I'm believing that GOD will cause a hunger to intensify in us all for the more of Him; that this time will help us to trust Him for every area of our lives. I believe He's able, In Jesus' Mighty Name.

Additional instructions:

1. Matthew 6:16-18 (anoint your face with oil and fix your countenance)
2. Morning Prayer (Psalm 63, Psalm 88:13)
3. Commit to studying the scriptures (II Timothy 2:15)
4. Drink a lot of water and apple juice, or cranberry juice (these juices need to be 100%) When you feel hungry, you should pray and worship the LORD so that your focus isn't on the hunger but it's on the power of GOD and His grace in your life.
5. Prepare a time daily 3xs a day where you devote for prayer, devotion and real bible study. If we are to get the victory over our flesh we have to jump deep in the word of GOD.

I pray for you and your spirit man to conquer your flesh in VICTORY... I stand with you in the HOLY GHOST and I declare GOD's grace, power and strength in you. I thank GOD that as we consecrate our lives to GOD we will experience clarity and freedom, answers to prayers and miracles in the name of JESUS. Thank You, Jesus our savior, be merciful to us.. receive our offering in Your name. Bind the hand of Satan in Jesus' Name.. I declare VICTORY in every area of our lives. Thank You Lord. Thank You and bless Your Mighty Name, Amen.

This is just a template that the Lord inspired me to give to my team, but I want you to customize it and make a decision to consecrate your soul to the Lord. God wants a deeper level of surrender out of you. Every time someone in Scripture decided to surrender in a deep way, God manifested his glory like never before.

I SURRENDER ALL

When Jacob wrestled the angel, he determined, "I will not let you go until you bless me." It was that determination that pushed Jacob to encounter God in a way that he would've never encountered Him if he gave up the fight when he got tired. Listen, the enemy has been trying to weaken your faith by bringing trials and tribulations your way that appear to be too much for you. Although it sounds cliché, God will never put more on you than you can bear. He will uphold you. He will strengthen you. He will guide you and provide for you, because you are His and he is yours. This is why consecration will help. When the issues of life try to overwhelm us, consecrate your soul and turn down the noise of the heathen voices. Turn down the sirens of the enemy. Turn down the background sound effects of life, and be still. Be still so that you can hear God clearly. Be still so that you can listen for his instructions. He may not come in the fire. He may not speak through the prophet. Sometimes, he will speak in a still small voice, but if our souls are not aligned, we will miss Christ on the way to church.

Jacob surrendered his whole soul, and as a result, God changed his name and birthed the twelve tribes through his loins. Mary surrendered all to God, with all of her questions, and God did a miracle through her that he has never done again. Joshua was afraid to lead after Moses died, but God gave him the courage and assurance with these words," I am with you"(Joshua 1:9) Soon after, God began to show himself mightily through Joshua's life. The three Hebrew boys gave God a complete YES and as a result, the King wanted them dead. But they declared in the face of death, "we still will not bow because the Lord is able to bring us out." Their faith was strengthened because their soul was surrendered. Paul and Silas were praising and praying in jail. Most of us would've been crying, "Lord, free me." But they had a revelation that God was bigger than the prison they were in. They were confident in the God who could bring them out, whenever he wanted to. When you consecrate your mind, body, and soul, you see the world differently. You see life differently. You see your role as a worship leader differently. You don't sing for attention. You minister with conviction. You don't preach for an honorarium. You point to Christ because he is the only one who is honorable. When you live a consecrated soul, you won't feel comfortable in certain places. When you live as a consecrated soul, you will automatically remove yourself from certain people. When you live as a consecrated soul, you may be isolated but the good news is, you are insulated. The angel of the Lord guides and protects you. He favors you with his love and kindness, and best of all, you can bask in the glory of God without interruption.

I want to challenge you to consecrate yourself to the Lord. If after 7 days, or 21 days, or 40 days, nothing has changed, then you can use that season as an experiment gone wrong and never consecrate again. But if something changes in your posture; if God does something in your heart; if God gives you songs in the night and a Word from on high, then that will be a sign that God is calling you deeper to give you greater.

Give yourself away. God is waiting to take you to another level in Him.

CHAPTER TEN
You are God's Distribution Center

Finally, brethren, whatsoever things are true, whatsoever things are honest, whatsoever things are just, whatsoever things are pure, whatsoever things are lovely, whatsoever things are of good report; if there be any virtue, and if there be any praise, think on these things.
(Philippians 4:8)

What does it mean to be a blessing? I think many of us automatically assume that blessings are monetary, material, or big houses and cars. But technically, to be a blessing means that you are willing to prevent misfortune to others. You are willing to remove yourself from the platform so that God can be lifted up. You are willing to celebrate someone else, instead of craving self-congratulation.

Most of what we do as God's leaders has all to do with knowing who we are. When you know who you are, you know what you are supposed to do. And I believe that, all throughout the Scriptures, God spent more time telling us who we are in different ways, so that we wouldn't settle for a carbon copy of somebody else. Jesus said, "you are salt and light." Salt was created to season. Light was created to illuminate. David said, "you are fearfully and wonderfully made." That means, you are supposed to be unique. You are supposed to bring something different to the table. One of the things that concerns me about worship leadership today is that everyone sounds the same. We adopt a way of singing that mirrors the person we like most, instead of seeing them as a mentor but maintaining your own unique gift. You are fearfully and wonderfully made. So, enjoy the person you look up to; but don't become the person you look up to. Joshua had to be Joshua. He couldn't stand in his anointing trying to sound like Moses. David had to be authentically David. He couldn't wear Saul's armor and win the battle. He had to be himself. All throughout Scripture we see that God wants us to know who we are and be who we are.

In order to remain available for His use, and in order to continue being a gift God wants to distribute, you've got to dwell in the presence of the Lord.

If I had to add to the wonderful metaphors that Scripture gives us about our identity and call, I would say this: God's will for our lives is to be a distribution center. We have been given gifts and talents for a reason, and the primary purpose is not to get rich off of your gifts. It's to give those gifts away to the world as reflections of God's love to his people. Ask yourself this question. When was the last time you did anything to help anyone? Have you asked GOD to give you an abundance so that you can be the pitcher that pours into empty cups? You are not a bank unto yourself. You are God's distribution center.

2 Corinthians 9:11 says that God wants to enrich us so we can be generous. This is why we sing, "All things come from thee oh Lord and of thine own have we given thee" (I Chronicles 29:14b). It's when you realize that you are absolutely, positively nothing without God that God will fill you up to the point that your anointing will overflow into the hearts and souls of others. But how can he fill you if you have nothing inside of your cup?

This is why Psalm 119:11 declares, "Thy Word Have I hid in my heart, that I might not sin against you." And Psalm 40:8 says, "I desire to do your will O my God; And Your law is within my heart(NIV)." These are passages that should help you to walk in the victory of Jesus in every area of your life. These are passages that will continue to fill your storehouse with the oil you need to live and lead. It's impossible to pour into people from an empty place. It's even more difficult to live a life of holiness if the Word of God has become an endangered species to you. In order to remain available for His use, and in order to continue being a gift God wants to distribute, you've got to dwell in the presence of the Lord. That doesn't mean sing all day. That doesn't mean preach all night. That means bask in the Word of the Lord. Let the word of God wash over you as often as possible.

The Bible says in Psalm 119:105, "Your Word is a lamp to my feet and a light for my pathway." The best way to ensure that you will walk out into the world with clarity and perspective is to daily commit to reading his Word. The word of God is the lamp that will help you to see. Micah 6:8 says, "He has showed you, O man, what is good. And what does the LORD require of you? To act justly and to love mercy and to walk humbly with your God." I'd ask you, as you prepare your time of prayer, that you would do self-inventory of what the will of God is in your life at home, work, church, and in your family. Pray that the Lord would show you how to handle the order of God and the power of God because, I believe sometimes we go through unnecessary things because we refuse to humble ourselves to leadership and the authorities that God has placed in our lives. "Oh what peace we often forfeit and oh what needless pains we bare. And, it's all because we do NOT carry everything to GOD in prayer"

As God's distribution center, you must remember that the freshness of the oil is dependent on the freshness of the fruit. If your fruit is not fresh, it will affect the atmosphere you are called to shift. If your fruit is not fresh, it may sicken the saints who are waiting for what God has placed in you. How do we freshen our fruit? Quite simply: through spending time in fellowship with the presence of the Lord. Paul the servant of Jesus says in Philippians 3:10, "That I may know Him and the power of His resurrection, and the fellowship of His sufferings, being conformed to His death,"

This scripture speaks to me in a place where it provokes me and pulls me to want to be closer to GOD in a real way. I'm not talking about anything spooky or crazy. But I'm referring to being a person that possesses the power of GOD. In Acts 5, there is an occurrence that happens with Apostle Peter. The Bible says that as Peter walked, his shadow healed the sick. This happened because of the power of GOD that was on his life. This happened because Peter understood the importance of private communion for a public demonstration. My prayer is that all of us, singers, musicians, teachers, support staff that we will walk and operate in that same power; so that people can be ensured of an encounter with GOD because of THE GOD that lives in us.

You've read this in previous chapters and I want to lift it up again. Every one of us who serve as leaders in the LORD'S church, need to be filled with the HOLY GHOST. Every one us should know how to pray in the spirit. This is so important especially during times of spiritual warfare, Altar call, prayer and intercession, the laying on of hands and when special needs are communicated. It's that power in GOD through the HOLY GHOST that will give us OVERCOMING POWER to ensure VICTORY in every situation. If you are God's distribution center, you must ready at all times to do what God has put you in the earth to do!

As you consume this information, I want you to pray that God would stir up the gift of the Holy Ghost in you. I want you to pray for power and evidence that will make a difference in your life. I want you to know that you are a threat to the kingdom of darkness. Don't be preoccupied with foolishness. Follow God with every fiber of your being. You may not know it, but you are in the place of consideration. What do I mean by that? It's very simple. God said to Satan, "Have you considered my servant Job." And in the same way, God has asked Satan if he has considered you. You are in the place of consideration. You have accumulated stock in the heavenly places of God. The enemy wants to see you defeated. But in the midst of pressure, don't whine. Don't complain. Don't compete. Don't gossip. Just worship. Roll up your sleeves and make a firm decision that you will make a difference. Don't be tossed to and fro by every wind of doctrine. Instead, be strong in the Lord and in the power of his might. For the bible says, "Many are the afflictions of the righteous, but the Lord delivers them out of them all." No doubt, there will be situations in our lives that come to us, but they won't over take us. Especially when we are operating in the power of the HOLY GHOST. The HOLY GHOST is an active intercessor between God, through our Lord Jesus Christ and us. When the Holy Spirit is present, victory is guaranteed. Blessings are guaranteed. Favor is guaranteed. Deliverance is guaranteed. This is why the power of the Spirit is so integral to your call as God's leader. You are not leading by yourself. The "I AM" is

> If you are God's distribution center, you must ready at all times to do what God has put you in the earth to do!

with you. The Holy Spirit is in you. The power of God is on you. And the greater you surrender to his power, the more he will cleanse and refresh you. I don't know about you, but I believe we are about to experience some of the freshest encounters in GOD in the next few years. I believe that God is raising up new front-liners who take God at his word—people of communion, not celebrity, who want the glory not the fame. I believe there will be a great shift before God comes back for his church; and I believe we will be the generation that initiates the shift. We will be the generation that yearns for the latter rain of God. We will be the generation that will fast and pray, and seek God's face. We will be the people that God can trust with the weight of his glory.

And to whom much is given, much is required. So, as Ephesians says, gird yourself in truth. Prepare yourself for battle. Prepare to be talked about. Prepare to be misunderstood. Prepare to suffer through seasons of isolation. Prepare to be overlooked. But know this: all things are working together for the good to them who love God; and to those who are called according to his purpose.

When I think back to the distribution analogy, I can't help but to think about the process that packaging the right product requires. Before we see the end result of a thing in the store, or on the shelves, it has been processed in a far-away factory, and each piece, ingredient, and component has been intricately selected so that every product reflects the manufacturer. In the kingdom of God, we are pressed but not in despair; we are crushed but not forsaken; we are cast down but not destroyed. We may have to go through the fire, but we are never going to burn because the one who can calm the sea and the storm, is able to extinguish every fire. God knows how hot to make the situation so that he can purify the ingredients that he needs to use during another season. And the beautiful thing about God, is that when he presents us on the shelf of life, we don't look like what we've been through. People will never know the pressing, and the breaking, and the crushing you survived. All they will know and see is the glory that is working through you.

I want to speak prophetically to every person reading this book. I want you to know that I hear the sound of victory over your life. I declare that the season of dead weight and excuses are over. This is the hour of REFRESHING. In Amos 3:3 the bible declares, "how can two walk together except we agree?" This is the hour of agreement. This is the hour to remove all unnecessary weights. This is the hour to come together so that the express will of God can be done.

You are not leading by yourself. The "I AM" is with you. The Holy Spirit is in you. The power of God is on you.

I heard the question asked recently, "HOW BAD DO YOU WANT IT"? Only you can answer that. Only you know how long you've been waiting for God to seal the deal in your life. Only you know how desperate you've been to see a real breakthrough happen in your life. But I believe that God has ripened you with revelation for this moment. I believe that God has allowed you to experience enough rejection in past seasons, so you can receive the blessing in this season. Hebrews 1:1-4 says this, "God, who at various times and in various ways spoke in time past to the fathers by the prophets, has in these last days spoken to us by His Son, whom He has appointed heir of all things, through whom also He made the worlds; who being the brightness of His glory and the express image of His person, and upholding all things by the word of His power, when He had by Himself purged our sins, sat down at the right hand of the

Majesty on high, having become so much better than the angels, as He has by inheritance obtained a more excellent name than they."

I want you to know that God has not forgotten about you. I know you may have thought that God had pushed you away, but God was preserving you for such a time as this. God is so concerned about you that He is speaking to you by the word of HIS power and by the power of HIS WORD. He, GOD, loves you so much that Christ has given you access to his heart, wisdom and power. Whatever you do, take full advantage of the GOD who cares for you. Remember, we are called to be in the spirit of unity from day to day. We are called to love each other as Christ loves us. We are called to be effective, not offensive. We are honored to work in his church, but not at the expense of communing with Him.

The scripture declares that, "In His presence there is fullness of JOY and at HIS right hand are pleasures for ever more." The fullness is the part of God that makes us desire the heart and the essence of God. It's this part of God that burns the foolishness off of our flesh and conforms it to the image of God. It's a daily process. Distribution is a daily process. It's not normal to just want the things of God unless you rehearse them daily. This is why years ago, I wrote a song that says, Through the eyes of faith I see God's grace through the eyes of Faith. The word is clear that faith comes by hearing and hearing by the word of the LORD. So we have to mature our will and our nature to practice God's word in order to become supernatural agents of his will. When we do that, God's presence will illuminate in us as we continue to study Him. Many times, we hear people say, "practice makes perfect" but that is so not true. Perfection and development will only come when we master the excellence of practicing with precision.

CHAPTER ELEVEN
Cultivating a Transformative Worship Department

How can two walk together except they agree. (Amos 3:3)

I am humbled when I think about the countries I've visited, and the invitations I've received all across the globe to encounter God with so many wonderful people. I am honored to take up my cross daily and follow Christ, knowing that the gift I have is not of myself; but it is solely because of the wonder-working power of an Almighty God. As I travel, I am often asked to give advice for worship departments who are struggling to be everything God has called them to be. I am typically asked to speak on worship from a local church perspective, and to share what I think is missing in the church today.

While much of this book has talked about the spiritual component of sanctification and communion, I believe another aspect that is missing from our worship departments is agreement and without it, it will be virtually impossible to succeed. Every church needs agreement. Every department needs agreement. Every team needs agreement, and the same is true in the worship department. In the worship ministry there must be an agreement that supersedes attendance and skill set. There must be agreement in the spirit, and agreement in the natural. By that I mean, we must all be willing participants (not employee-minded), eager to see the glory of the Lord manifest in his house. We must agree on that one objective even if we disagree about who should lead which song; even if we disagree about how many fast songs to sing and how many slow songs to sing; even if we have differences of opinion about the order of service, everyone who is a member of the worship department (from the director, to the musicians, to the singers, dancers, and greeters) should agree that the primary goal is to get to God. This is the spiritual component that is essential for every worship department to work.

Agreement does not mean every person on your team will be best friends. It doesn't mean you should go out to eat every Sunday after church. Fellowship is important, don't get me wrong, but what is most important is that you know those among whom you labor. You'd be surprised how many people try to lead a house into the presence of the Lord with people who are absolute strangers to them. They don't know their names. They don't know their family dynamic. They don't know anything about them except what role they play or what voice part they sing. In the natural, we need agreement. We need to know one another. We need to care about each other. We need to respond when one of our team members is in pain. We need to rejoice with those who rejoice. We need to be an extended family to one another, not just volunteers who complete a task without any invested interest in being the body of Christ that God has called us to be. Saints of God, there must be agreement. The glory of God doesn't manifest in confusion and disunity.

Every person appointed to the worship ministry must be a person who is subject to the leading of the Holy Spirit. You must agree with God, and agree with others. As a leader, you must have consistent fellowship with GOD in His word, through prayer, and by discerning the things of GOD. You, yourself, must be subject to leadership.

This is a touchy subject nowadays because everybody wants a team to be submitted to him or her, but nobody wants to submit to their leader. Everybody wants management, hair and makeup, stylists, and a traveling background band, but who are you submitted to? Who are you receiving from? What table are you eating from? How do we know that you are worthy of the team you are asking for? Without agreeing to submit to some pastoral presence/mentor in your life, you will quickly disintegrate. Your voice may be amazing, but your soul will be in trouble. Your mind may be fully functioning, but your heart will eventually break down. We need agreement. All of us need to make sure that systems of agreement, unity, and teamwork are put in place so that everybody understands that we are all in this for one purpose: to make His name glorious. If you insist on agreement in the spirit, agreement in the natural, and agreement to submit to your leader, then the Judas' and the Aiken's in the camp will quickly manifest. You will see who is who based on how they respond to the challenge of agreement.

> ...everybody wants a team to be submitted to him or her, but nobody wants to submit to their leader. Everybody wants management, hair and makeup, stylists, and a traveling background band, but who are you submitted to?

After a theology of agreement is put in place at your church, then here are a few suggestions to build, cultivate and sustain a transformative worship department.

Introduction: Each member, before enlisting in the

worship ministry, must be introduced to the department. Each member needs to know the purpose, passion, and theology of your department. You need to make it very clear what this is and what it is not. This, for example, is a place of servitude, not entitlement. This is a place where intercessors who yearn for the pure presence of GOD will be responsible for leading others into the free-flowing glory of the most High God. Individuals must be called and committed to praying for the Pastor, Leaders and the congregation as a whole. He or she must know how serious the role of worship is to building up the spiritual reinforcements of a people and defeating the enemies of hell. An introduction to your ministry will clear the misconceptions, and allow everyone to understand what they are signing up for.

Audition: After the introduction has been made, there must be an organized audition that follows the biblical structure and observation of the skill set and vocal ability. In 1 Chronicles 15:22,27, Chenaniah was appointed by King David as the Chief Music minister. His role was to assess the ability of the Levites. There must be something in place that helps determines where people serve most effectively in a ministry that is attempting to honor GOD in excellence.

Interview: Next, there should be an interview. The purpose of the interview process is to hear the heart of the person, and to get a clear understanding of their relationship with God. As their leader, you must understand who GOD is to them and what His assignment is for their lives. The worst thing is to link up with someone you don't know. The Bible says in Luke 6:45, " A good man out of the good treasure of his heart brings forth good; and an evil man out of the evil treasure of his heart brings forth evil. For out of the abundance of the heart his mouth speaks." The heart space is very important. What someone says about their lives says a lot about what's in their heart. Proverbs 4:23, " Keep your heart with all diligence, For out of it springs the issues of life"

In my interview, I ask questions like:
1. What is your private devotional time like?
2. What are you reading now?
3. When was the last time you led someone to Christ?

Observation: I believe that after the audition and the interview, there needs to be clear alignment with the leadership of the church. I believe that all worship leaders should do the following:

1. Tithe and give offerings (Malachi 3:11 and 2Cor 9:6-9)
2. Study to develop their lives as Disciples of Christ (2Tim 2:15)
3. Be a person of prayer
4. Have a morally clean life

In order to have a vibrant worship ministry, there must be *purity, skillfulness, anointing, order,* and *unity.* A pure spirit will bring about change and cause God to take notice. To be skillful means that you exercise the discipline of being a student. To have the anointing means you understand that above your gift is the call to heal and bring deliverance. Through the anointing comes influence. And ultimately, the anointing will destroy yokes and lift burdens. To be orderly means to know your place in the role you have been called to occupy. I Chronicles 6:31 says," And these are they that

David set over the service in the house of the Lord. Then they waited on their office according to their order" To be unified means that every person plays their part, recognizing that their part is important but it is not the only part that matters. Psalms 100:5 says, "Enter into his gates with thanksgiving and enter his courts with praise; be thankful unto him and bless His name." When your worship team is unified, they will be able to march together, sing together, and worship together in such a way that strength and victory become consistently predictable outcomes.

RESTORATION

I believe God's house needs restoration. I believe restoration needs to begin in the area of worship. For too long, we have allowed foolishness to reign in sacred spaces, but God is giving us another chance to change the filter. He's giving us another chance to clean our houses and to clean our hearts. As you prepare your worship department, let your first prayer be, "Lord, how can we restore the ministry of worship back in your house?" Don't get caught up in what other people are doing at their church. Don't let the spirit of competition grip your mind. Instead, focus on building a steady foundation. Put systems in place that will work even when you're absent. Establish order and harmony with the overall vision that your overseeing pastor has shared with you. Give structure to those who need it. In I Kings, we are told that the singers, musicians and the Levitical Priests were compensated through the tithe and offerings of the Church in order that they might stay focused on serving the house of the Lord. If

If the Levites aren't tithing into the house, then they don't deserve compensation from the house.

the Levites aren't tithing into the house, then they don't deserve compensation from the house.

Establish order. Be willing to let some people go. God will raise up a Joshua, a David, or a Miriam in due season. Just push past your issues and watch GOD do the impossible.

Pray This Prayer

The Prayer

Oh holyJesus. My Savior Jesus
Reach down and make me whole
O blessed Jesus, The mighty Jesus
Please wash me and Yes make me whole
Please wash me and Yes heal this soul, oh my troubled soul
Wash me and yes make me whole

Amen

CHAPTER TWELVE
The Seed of David

How can two walk together except they agree. (Amos 3:3)

Some years before I decided to write this book, I put together a conference called the "Seed of David." I want to end this book by sharing with you my address that I gave at that conference. In it you will read the passion, the purpose, and the point to all that you have read and why. It is my prayer that we study the life of David, his mistakes, his forgiveness, his prayers, his honesty, and his transparency; because David shifted the entire paradigm of worship. David was God's anointed vessel called to a place that no one had ever gone, to do something that no one had ever done. I believe you are called to do the same, and it is my prayer that you achieve all that God has for you—without delay, frustration, or unwarranted challenges. Here is an excerpt of my opening remarks for the "Seed of David" conference.

> Thank you all for coming to participate in an event of worship that has been in my heart space for some time. THE SEED OF DAVID...It's not a conference but it's a gathering of minds and hearts of people who have an express desire to come to know Jesus and his attributes in a more intimate way. It's a place where challenges are presented amongst friends and family members of the KING of Glory. This short time is designed for

you to take an introspective look inside your personal relationship with God and the assignment of God on your life without any distractions and hindrances of any kind. It's a place of accountability. So you will have to make decisions that will determine where you will go as a person of worship. Everyone here isn't a Musician, Praise and Worship Leader or a Worship Pastor. But all of you feel some sense of a tug from the heart of GOD to consider the whole matter as it relates to the ASSIGNMENT and DESTINY of GOD for your life.

I have deliberately invited people who I believe I'm called to assist in the journey of discovering the will of GOD in worship for your individual lives both on the platform of service and in your personal space. Let me start off with this disclaimer and don't forget this: I DON'T HAVE THE PATTERN ON WORSHIP BUT GOD HAS BEEN TRE MENDOUSLY KIND TO ME BY TEACHING ME HIS HEART. In this short time spent, we will engage in conversations that will cause you, I pray, to desire clarity in the Holy Ghost, clarity that can be articulated and justified in and through the word of GOD. This call to the worship ministry doesn't make you better than; it makes you responsible for...Every person who assists in the worship service in the CORPORATE SETTING has the responsibility to ensure that the waiting congregation has what I call A GOD ENCOUNTER. This time is only designed to scratch the surface for you and in you. It will not and cannot quench the thirst that you will acquire for the more of God through Jesus.

You will hear words like Assignment, Destiny and Integrity during your visit here and I want you to be CLEAR on the differences in them all. It will help you in the never-ending journey of fulfilling the purposes of God for your life. There will be a time where we ask questions and as best I can, I will speak from my own well and experiences and will assist you.

I'm sure you ask why the Seed of David and I want to support this by simply saying I used David but if we probe the lives of many called and used men of GOD in the scripture they all had MAJOR ISSUES to overcome. I chose David because in spite of all of his issues, he still had a never dying passion to please the very heart of God. He was jacked up! But he knew how to repent and cry out to God for RESTORATION and CLARITY.

I want to officially ask you to create your own out line that works best for you. However it works for you to take and eat it and live in it, do that.

In the Old Testament scripture:
Ezekiel 3 & Ezekiel 33 Being in fellowship with God in worship privately is so hard to do in this day and time because we are so distracted by so many things. There are powers and principalities that pull for God-space and God-time. Just think about: how many of you can go anywhere with out your cell phone, your iPad or your media device. Often even in corporate worship we can't connect with what could be a pure God moment because we have allowed these little

devices to become A PIECE OF OUR PASSION. To some degree I understand when you're job requires it, but come on ya'll... Really? In our worship (either private or in a corporate setting) we are getting out of hand.

What does the word of God actually mean in Romans 8:38,39 For I am persuaded that neither death nor life, nor angels nor principalities nor powers, nor things present nor things to come, nor height nor depth, nor any other created thing, shall be able to separate us from the love of God which is in Christ Jesus our Lord.

Where is our allegiance? Is our commitment to God not more important and sacred than a text, a tweet or a facebook post? I'm guilty of it too so I don't speak from a posture of elevated grandeur. But, my rule of thumb is... if you're sick God has to heal you, if you're dead I can't help you.

The Assignment
An Assignment is different than Purpose, Destiny, Calling & Passion. It has a DEADLINE. You have to meet the moment with obedience & accuracy

The Destiny the bible says in Jeremiah 29:11, "I know the thoughts I have toward you, says the LORD, thoughts of peace and not of evil, to give you a future and a hope."(NJKV). It's the thing or things you live and breathe with ease. It's the reason you were born. There will always be fruit

I want to ask you: what is your assignment? Are

you completing it? Are you delaying it? What is the thing that you live and breathe with ease? Where is the fruit of your labor?

In this season, God is calling us to be consecrated souls, not just talented singers. In order to lead the people of God into his presence, I've learned that people have to feel safe and trust that you will lead them to the presence of God or else they will just watch you. Don't lead praise and worship with a song, lead with your heart. Have integrity. Embrace structure and order. Don't get into a power struggle with the designs that were laid out by your leader. Your commitment is to God, not man . Worship is all about your heart and love for God . So, get to the place where we can be broken in God's presence.

As I close out the first volume of chapters for this first book, I wanted to end by showing you the beginning of my process. I didn't know that a small welcome address would grow into a book filled with 12 chapters of wisdom from above. I didn't know that God was using the seed of obedience then to water my future now. If I didn't know that God had this up his sleeve, I wonder what God has for you on the other side of obedience. I wonder what God wants to bring you to, and bring you through, if you'd only believe him, come to yourself, and return to the Father. Return to revival. Return to wrestling with God until he blesses you. Return to sanctifying yourself in his presence so that your private practice will bring a public demonstration of God's glory. You are God's workmanship. He has anointed you to change the landscape of worship for his glory. But the change begins in you. The change begins in me. Transformation will happen in our churches when it begins to happen in our families. I pray that God will continue to transform you through the words written on these pages. I pray that you will be richly blessed in all that you do, and that God will establish you to shift the kingdom for His glory.

THE WORSHIP LEADERS
Benediction

Now unto him who can cause us all to stand
present us faultless at his throne yet once again
I pray life receives the change and your soul be
rearranged
by His power as His Glory is revealed

Now unto Him who can do exceedingly
Abundantly that is the power that works in me
Allow your life to be set free
May you walk in victory
by His power as His Glory is revealed

This is my prayer to you no matter where you are.

I pray the Lord would grace you with his mantle

That His strength would be come perfect in your weakness

That as you stand before God's people from every walk
of life that you take this assignment as an apostolic
appointment

That you would allow the Lord to release His anointing in
you

Fresh oil Fresh strength, renewed strength like never before

My sister and my brother as you stand before God's people that you would say unto his people what thus says the Lord

I pray that he would charge your ears with sensitivity and that he would give you songs in the night.. In the Name of Jesus

Be it unto you. Receive it in the name of the Lord. Fresh dimension,Heights unseen in the name of the Lord.

And it is so, and we believe it by faith

And we decree it from nation to nation, heart to heart transformation, restoration lives changed, transformed, metamorphosis. Never ever again the same in the name of Jesus

In the name of the Lord, Hallelujah to Jesus

New dimensions in Jesus ...Hallelujah to Jesus ..You'll never be the same again

Hallelujah to him. He's able to do it.. Exceedingly and abundantly in the name of Jesus

And it is so

And it is so

Be it unto you according to your faith

Allow the Lord to enlarge himself in you

In the name of Jesus
In the Name of Jesus

GO in peace and provide for the world the sound of the Kingdom

APPENDIX

Here are some amazing books that will be a blessing to your life and ministry.

The Power & Purpose of Praise & Worship
        by Myles Munroe
The Power of Praise & Worship
        by Terry Law
The Praise & Worship BIBLE
He Came To Set The Captives Free
        by Rebecca Brown

ACKNOWLEDGEMENTS

I'd like appreciate and thank my Dad, Maurice C. Hurd, Sr.; my sisters Sharon, Michelle and my brother Maury for letting me be unmistakably me. Most people would never believe I could be "dramatic or Extra" but they know and know it well. Special thanks to my Pastor Dr. John K. ,Sr and Pastor Trina Jenkins; the Elders and the entire First Baptist Church of Glenarden for allowing me the privilege to serve you for these last 14years. It's been a journey that has shaped my entire life.

Pastor Jenkins, thanks for trusting me and believing in me and not my gift. I can't thank you enough for the many deposits you've made in my LIFE, my HEART and my CALLING. To my Minister of Music, Dr. Shirley M.K Berkeley, you are the best example of faithfulness I've ever seen. I'm grateful you trusted me to partner with you and serve you. I thank GOD for my team and staff— the amazing Anthony Brown who is taking the globe by storm with his amazing gift to capture God's songs that cause all of use to hear heaven; thanks to my band and my co workers who allow me the privilege to serve you. Thank you Justin Robinson for your photography, Kym Lee for wardrobe and Arthur Lee for assisting me as my barber.

I thank GOD for all my mentors, Bishop George Searight, Dr. Judy McAllister and my sister who transitioned too soon, Elder Renetha Macklin—your lives have impacted me forever. Special thanks to all of the many young worship leaders who allow me the honor of pouring some nuggets God gave me into your life. Thanks a million to my Godmother, Rev. Dr. Thomasina Portis, Ma Francis Brooks, the late Barbara Boyd and Lady Many Dozier. You guys would always speak life over me and pull me in from being in my own way. I want to thank GOD for all the Pastors and Ministers of Music that have allowed me the opportunity to minister around the world.

ABOUT THE AUTHOR

Over the last two decades, Stephen Hurd has distinguished himself as one of the leading voices in urban praise and worship music and his songs "Revelations 19:1," "Undignified" and "Lead Me To The Rock" are sung at faith gatherings around the globe. His sixth and most recent CD was designed as a tool to inspire men to take on a greater leadership role in conducting worship as the faithful assemble and for that role to make a residual impact on their personal lives and community.

"In the Old Testament it was always men who led the worship," Hurd offers. "I think wives trust the God in their husband more when they see that their husband really loves God and is not ashamed to worship him. I think sons respect and want to be like their father if they see that he's a man loving God and regulating things in our house and creating a healthy environment. I think families will be stronger when men understand their place in the worship community and not follow the lead of their wives."

The Brandywine, MD-bred psalmist has been singing since childhood. His inspirations back then were R&B crooners Jeffrey Osborne and Peabo Bryson. "I love the rich tones of their voices," he recalls. "I marveled at Larnelle Harris as a technique builder for me. Then, I heard Marvin Winans and was in amazement. I grew up with it all: R&B, gospel and then classical music." He channeled that love of music as a student at the Duke Ellington School of the Arts and continued to perfect it as music major at Howard University. He then taught music at various high schools in the Maryland area. On the weekends, he served as music director for the late Rev. Donald Vails' DC Choral Kaleidoscope and also

The Capital City Mass Youth Choir. He eventually left teaching and became a music minister with various Washington, D.C. area churches before settling in at First Baptist of Glenarden. Along the way, he also self-produced two well-received independent CDs before he came to the attention of Integrity Music.

Hurd wasn't actively seeking a record deal but his Howard University classmate James Walker, who went on to become an entertainment attorney, passed one of his CDs on to Al Hobbs, who was chairman of the Gospel Music Workshop of America (GMWA). Hobbs then passed it to Jackie Patillo. "Several people told me about Stephen," recalls Patillo who was A&R Director at Integrity Music at the time. "Al Hobbs was the first. Stephen has the heart and soul of a worshiper and it was a privilege to facilitate his music ministry." She trekked up to Washington, D.C. to watch him lead Sunday morning praise and worship at First Baptist and was sold. Over the next six years, Hurd released the best-selling CDs *A Call To Worship*, *My Destiny* and *Times of Refreshing*.

In spite of his Integrity success, Hurd quietly pondered launching a label for a while as he watched various peers become successful as independent artists. "I was afraid to do it because I had never done it before," he says. "I'm a creative mind, not a business mind." However, Hurd's developed a business mind and pulled all the pieces to this musical mission together and created a timeless project to stand the test of time and to transform a new generation of men into worshippers. "I never had a B plan," says Hurd. "My A Plan was to do Music ministry or something arts related." Fortunately, Plan A is working out just fine.

STEPHEN HURD
FACTS & FIGURES

CD DISCOGRAPHY

2012	*O That Men Would Worship*	Hurd The Word	N/A
2009	*Times of Refreshing*	Integrity	#8 Top Gospel Albums
2006	*My Destiny*	Integrity	#11 Top Gospel Albums
2004	*A Call To Worship*	Integrity	#15 Top Gospel Albums
2001	*In The Overflow Vol. 2*	Hurd The Word	N/A
1999	*Corporate Worship Vol. 1*	Hurd The Word	N/A

RADIO SINGLES

2008	*Amazing*	Integrity	N/A
2007	*Destiny*	Integrity	#24 Hot Gospel Songs
2007	*Great Praise*	Integrity	#17 Hot Gospel Songs
2005	*Lead Me To The Rock*	Integrity	#22 Hot Gospel Songs
2004	*Undignified*	Integrity	Top 10 Radio Hit

GUEST CD APPEARANCES

2010   *Your Name Alone* (from Various Artists CD "Gotta Have Gospel, Vol. 8")

2007   *You Are The Lord* (from Tyrone Powell's CD "Inside Out")

2005   *Lead Me to the Rock* (from Various Artists CD "Stellar Awards Hits 2005")

2005   *Todah* (from Various Artists CD "Gospel Today Presents: Praise & Worship III")

2003   *There is None Like You* (from Various Artists CD "Art of Praise")

STELLAR AWARDS

2010   Praise & Worship CD of the Year – Times of Refreshing (Win)
2008   Praise & Worship CD of the Year – My Destiny (Nominated)

DOVE AWARDS

2005   Contemporary Gospel Recorded Song – Undignified (Nominated)

TELEVISION APPEARANCES

2011   Bobby Jones Gospel (BET)
2008   Praise The Lord (TBN)
2008   Allstate Gospel Superfest (Syndicated)
2005   Gospel of Music with Jeff Majors (TV One)

SPECIAL APPEARANCE
2009   Had the distinct honor of singing for President Barak Obama in
        the Oval office

ALL CHART REFERENCES ARE BILLBOARD MAGAZINE